"Enjoy this new book from Jeannie S
deeply personal vignettes from her l
solid Bible study and practical ways for everyone to get involved
in introspection, biblical instruction, and hopefully healing."
DR. FRANK PAGE
Pastor and Author

"In this book, Jeannie offers her vulnerability, inviting readers to
an incredible journey of healing. The truth? *The Gift* is a gift to
all of us!"
KIRK AND JENNIFER WALDEN
Authors and Speakers

"*The Gift* is honestly just that. It's a gift to those that will honestly
and openly read it. I live every day in the world of 'deliverance
ministry.' There are times that people get some freedom but
not full freedom because they miss important aspects that are
addressed in this book. It's a personal and practical journey to
understand the importance of being healed from the inside out.
It's a biblical journey that's laced with compassion for those that
have deep wounds and are seeking peace and restoration. It's a
book that speaks from experience and not just data gathering.
The Gift will bless you and will help you. As a matter of fact, it
will help many."
PASTOR GREG LOCKE
Pastor and Founder of Global Vision Bible Church, Mt. Juliet, Tennessee
Author and Speaker

"Someone said if you are looking to be restored to what you were
before you were broken, you are in recovery. But if you are looking to shed your old self and become a totally new self, you are
ready to be healed of your brokenness.

Jeannie Smith has found deep healing for her brokenness. In this book she invites others to join her in the healing journey. I agree with her suggestion on how to read this book. 'Don't just read, show up.' We can read looking for information (and there is good information available here). Or we can allow ourselves to be caught up in the flow of the text and receive what she is offering: spiritual and emotional and mental health and wholeness are all available to those who show up."

BROTHER FOUNT SHULTS

MA in Greek and Church History, PhD in Hebrew Language and Literature
Bible and Theology professor, Author, and Speaker

"A journey of pain that is raw and insightful that eventually softened parts of my own heart that I didn't know were hard. The path of forgiveness was clear and I could see myself in places of my life that could have been calmed by the way the ultimate gift would have soothed and filled the emptiness in my soul. This book exposes the ugliness that we unintentionally feel about ourselves and how and more importantly who can bring comfort and freedom. I would highly recommend this book."

NELLY ROACH

President, Choose Life Marketing

The

Gift

Embrace the Wonder
of Healing

JEANNIE SCOTT SMITH

The Gift

Published by Savage Press
PO Box 623307
Oviedo, Florida 32762
www.ahigherlife.com

ISBN: 9781958211106 (Paperback)
9781958211113 (ebook)

Library of Congress Control Number: 2022914735

Printed in the United States of America.

10 9 8 7 6 5 4 3 2 1

To my daddy, Thomas Eugene Scott. It was through the sorrow of losing you on December 27th, 2020, that I discovered the greatest gifts you ever gave me, some of which are even shared in this book by "Daddy's little girl." You are always in my heart. I love you, Daddy. Indeed, your love is "long lasting and far reaching."

To my grandmother, Mary Brown Hewitt, who entered into heaven during the publishing of this book on August 23rd, 2022. It is because of you that I am the woman I am today. What a legacy and gift you have left. We are all better because of you. "Who can find a virtuous woman? For her price is far above rubies" (Prov. 31:10 KJV). I love you, Grandma. I will always cherish my most precious memories with you.

To my beloved brother, Bennie Eugene Scott, whom also entered into heaven during the publishing of this book on October 6th, 2022. Your unexpected departure was almost more than I could bear. You were not just my brother; you were my friend. A special bond that's hard to comprehend. I'm so glad God gave you to me as a gift, if only for a little while. My heart longs to be with you again. I love you always, Sis.

Therefore, since we are surrounded by such a great cloud of witnesses, let us throw off everything that hinders and the sin that so easily entangles. And let us run with perseverance the race marked out for us, fixing our eyes on Jesus, the pioneer and perfector of faith...

—HEBREWS 12:1-2

Gift Contents

Acknowledgments

To my Lord and Savior, Jesus. It is You alone I first acknowledge and to whom I give all glory. Thank You for teaching me, and gifting me with truth and healing. Thank You for Your mercy and strength to accomplish the things to which You call me. Thank You for speaking life into me, forgiving me, loving me, and always calling me higher to immeasurably more than I could ever imagine.

To all the pioneers that have gone before me, thank you. Thank you for your obedience to God in writing Bible studies, and teaching material that has healed and trained so many. I am forever grateful to you and the miracle that healing has brought in my life. Your legacy will continue through others like me.

To all those who have been blessed already by the contents of this book, thank you. Thank you for trusting me and the Lord to lead you into a lasting healing. Thank you for inspiring me, and encouraging me to share this with others. Thank you for praying for me during the process.

Before We Begin . . .

This study will be filled with gifts! My love language is gifts, so each time you receive a gift as you travel through the pages, know that I am expressing my love for you. Of course, the greatest gift one can receive through grace, from God, is the gift of salvation. So, before we begin, if you have never had the opportunity to receive Jesus as your Lord and Savior, simply pray this:

> Lord, forgive me of my sins. Thank You for paying the ultimate price on the cross so that I may be forgiven and live eternally. I receive this gift and ask that You come into my heart and life and reign. I will follow You. In Jesus' name. Amen!

This short but anointed little book has been inspired by a Holy God to set you free! There is so much pain and brokenness in this world. Some pain we find ourselves living in may be from our own choices, and some pain comes from sources completely out of our control, but here is what I know: there is only one way to healing. Our circumstances and stories may differ, but there is only one God, one Savior who heals us all. His name is Jesus. By His stripes we are healed!

If you are reading this, it is your God-appointed time to hear His voice. He is coming after you with relentless love to heal and restore you. He reaches out to us all in many different ways. It could be through a book, Scripture, mentor, prayer, worship, a great sermon, nature, lyrics, or even a simple phone call from a friend. In this particular moment, I believe He is reaching out to you.

My story has many dynamics, one of which is abortion. I endured years of pain and then one day, God orchestrated a phone conversation between me and a woman who had helped others like me to heal. I remember being skeptical as we talked and I asked, "Is this really going to help me?" to which she replied, "Jeannie, oh yes! It will be the next best thing to your salvation." Now, I knew how much my salvation meant to me and I couldn't imagine this could compare, but you know what? She was right! I am so glad I was willing to accept the challenge of her response!

You see, I finally realized my need for healing and when I courageously took steps forward and trusted someone to strategically help me, miracles happened. Not only was I completely healed, but my identity was restored. Then God began to use me to inspire and change the lives of those around me by sharing some simple truths He taught me, and now I want to share them with YOU!

On a personal level, I have experienced a broken home as a child, through divorce and an absent father, then an unplanned pregnancy, an abortion, and depression. I have suffered from suicidal thoughts, infertility, financial hardships, endured marital conflicts, struggles of blended families, rejection, and betrayal. I have experienced grief at its deepest form through the loss of family members.

I have counseled other women also hurting from abortion, miscarriage, childhood trauma, sudden death of a child, general grief over a loved one, sexual trauma, all forms of abuse, suicide, and infidelity. I have also counseled teens as they navigate the dark peer pressure and pain they face daily in today's culture. Through it all, without knowing our identity, truth, and our significance in Christ, we will not make it, but if we have the right tools, we are absolutely going to emerge as champions over anything the enemy throws at us.

I share all of this to let you know I am experienced in the content I present. I cannot say I know exactly what you're going through, but I can say I *know* the one who does! His name is Jesus and He comes to present an invitation.

Come, My child. Do you want to be restored? To be truly healed?

Do you want your mirror to reflect an inner beauty that has been missing?

Do you want to find freedom and soar into great purpose?

Are you ready to receive your miracle?

If your answer is yes to any of these questions, you have identified a need for God's healing and redemption in your life. This is your appointed time. Oh, what joy!

> *He bore all my sins, all my griefs and all*
> *my sorrows. And yet there is a full tale*
> *yet to be fulfilled. I don't understand it.*
> *I simply affirm it. I accept it.*
> —ELIZABETH ELLIOT

If Christ lives in us, we never suffer alone. When we suffer,

He suffers along with us, but the truth is there is no transformational work done anywhere without suffering. So, it is then that the suffering produces a great reward. Yes! a gift.

> *Come now . . . says the Lord. No matter how*
> *deep the stain of your sins, I can remove it. I*
> *can make you as clean as freshly fallen snow.*
> *Even if you are stained as red as crimson, I*
> *can make you as white as wool. If you will*
> *only obey me and let me help you.*
> —ISAIAH 1:18–19 NLT

> *The Lord is close to the brokenhearted and*
> *saves those who are crushed in spirit.*
> —PSALM 34:18 NIV

Come now, embrace the wonder of healing.

The Unwrapping

Every good and perfect gift is from above,
coming down from the Father of the
heavenly lights.
—JAMES 1:17 NIV

I can still hear the sound of my heels tapping the floor as I pranced around the house in the pink pumps my grand-daddy bought me. He always wanted his baby doll to have a new pair of fancy shoes. I felt so grown up as I buckled the straps around my ankles. Across the room, my granddaddy proudly smiled at me as I showed off my new shoes. At this particular moment, I was convinced I was a princess and all my dreams were going to come true. Then, as time went on, pain struck. My family unit was destroyed. Sin entered into my life, I made mistakes, and brokenness consumed me.

My greatest pain was from abortion. I certainly didn't grow up wanting to have an abortion, but that is what happened. Then, all my dreams were truly shattered. I experienced years of hidden pain that made it difficult to even breathe, BUT GOD and His ever-present grace healed me!

You are about to embark on a journey! I remember the day I surrendered my broken heart to God and trusted a group of loving women to guide me through His Word. I remember feeling anxious, unsure of what was ahead, and questioning myself and others, "Do I really need this?" Let me tell you, it was life-changing! Yes, I did need it. By taking this step of faith you will be tremendously blessed and healed at the deepest level by our God!

As we prepare ourselves for this journey, let me share a little story with you. One day I was sitting, crying, rocking back and forth in an effort to comfort myself. I could see an image and I knew it was Jesus. In His hands, He was holding a gift. It was wrapped so beautifully. He began walking towards me and extending His hands for me to take the gift, but I recoiled. I knew He wanted me to have it, but I didn't feel worthy to accept it. He was such a gentleman. He didn't pressure me. He patiently waited. As He drew closer, I was so overwhelmed by His love for me that I finally reached out and fully received the gift. For a long time, I didn't speak of this encounter to anyone. I held it close to my heart. Today, I find myself inspired to share it with others, so I have titled this book *The Gift* because what God wants to give you is simply a gift. His Son, Jesus, bought you this gift many years ago. You just have to receive it!

Imagine yourself as a little girl. Your daddy has just given you a beautifully wrapped package. The ribbons on top are laced with sparkles. As you reach to release the bow, your heart is full of anticipation. What you hold in your hands is a special treasure, a gift personalized just for you! Together we are going to unwrap the gift and apply the contents to our lives. As we work through the contents you will discover a friend who connects with your heart and the most precious love letters from your heavenly Father, inspired just for you! I promise, this is a "no ordinary" Bible study about our extraordinary God and once you complete it, you will never be the same.

All I ask is that you show up and start! I encourage you to

work through one chapter a week so you can digest what you're reading. You are going to need a journal or notebook, Bible, and pen. Each week you will be given thoughts to ponder and questions to answer. Don't look ahead! Work on one chapter per week only. Stay faithful, because each week builds up to the next. Find someone you can trust to be your accountability partner. Ask this person to pray for you and to be a listening support. You may need additional support through the aid of a counselor. Seek help. Everyone is different and has different needs, so I highly recommend that you find the support system that's right for you. Work through *The Gift* at your own pace, take breaks as you need them, and allow what you're reading to soak in. Fully yield your heart to the work of the Lord in you. Don't hold back. This is your special time! Allow the tears to flow; He holds every one of them in a bottle declares Psalm 56. You don't have to be strong; He will be your strength. You just have to be obedient. You can trust Him. He is such a good, good Father. I will be honest with you, it will be tough at times, but the end result is oh, so worth it! You can count on these promises found in Isaiah 61:

There will be freedom for the captives,
a release from darkness.
He will comfort all who mourn,
and for those who grieve,
He will bestow on them a crown of beauty
instead of ashes,
the oil of joy
instead of mourning,
and a garment of praise
instead of a spirit of despair.
They will be called oaks of righteousness,

a planting of the Lord
for the display of His splendor.

Sweet Friend, I look forward to the miracle God performs in you. I pray you will enter into His rest. I pray you will swim in His grace. I pray He will restore your heart and give you great purpose and freedom in living!

In His Healing Love,

Jeannie

CHAPTER 1

Discovering Your Wound

The Father faithfully "heals the
brokenhearted and binds up their wounds."

—PSALM 147:3 NIV

I always felt haunted by my past. I mean, I knew God had forgiven me, but there was this lingering pain. It was as if something was missing, or incomplete. Then one day, I found myself sitting in front of a woman whom I did not know. I will never forget this encounter, because she asked me a question that changed my life. You see, I was meeting with her because I wanted to volunteer at a crisis pregnancy center. In my search for wholeness, I figured this must be what was missing! I needed to serve and help others. Her question was very simple: "Have you ever been *healed* from the pain of your abortion?"

This question left me puzzled. It was in this very moment that God started to teach me the difference between forgiveness and healing. God's forgiveness is instant, but healing is a process. God forgave me directly upon repentance, but the necessary healing had not yet taken place. Glory! I had finally discovered the missing piece!

The more I reflected, the more I realized I was in pretty bad shape. I held resentment and unforgiveness in my heart, causing me to be a bitter woman. The question posed to me that day made me dig deep enough to discover that most of my struggles were stemming from my wound. The emptiness and shame I carried kept me locked in a prison. My self-image was broken. I felt distorted. I thought my sense of

God's forgiveness is value had been restored when I accepted *instant, but healing* Christ, but there was still some unfin- *is a process.* ished work. Much healing still needed to take place. Does this need for healing resonate with your sense of groping for something more? I pray God will begin to give you insight into your need. I pray He gives you vision of His finished work in you!

I call you, Lord, and shy away, from all you have to give;
I dare to call you Father, and my spirit starts to live.
I can't conceive a Lordly One could ever care for me,
Or that the One who rules the world would die to set me free.
Yet when I call you Father and allow your love to flow;
Then all your might and majesty, you gently to me show.
You ask that I should trust you, a simple task it would seem;
Yet love I once was sure of, seems but a distant dream.
Why should it be so hard a task? to hold this love you've
    shown?
To simply bring to memory the promises I've known.
It seems a poor excuse, one I've no right to spout,
To say that all my hope and trust, has been replaced by doubt.
I do not doubt that God exists, and rules over land and sea;
But that this Lord Almighty should truly care for me.
A doubt that is quite unfounded, as I daily tend my tasks;
And find that God is always there, to help me when I ask.
His love is not condemning, though often I let Him down,

Yet if I look, His smile I see, not some expected frown.
His patience is longsuffering, and long He suffers me;
For all my fears and doubting, His love won't cease to be.
His love is never ending, He pours it from above,
And soaks this hurting child of His, in His cleansing, healing
   love.
No more I'll doubt nor stumble, a claim I long to make;
But 'tis only wishful thinking, such promises I'd break.
But trusting in His goodness, I'll edge ever slowly forward,
And try to place my doubts and fears, in the strong hands
   of my Lord.

—Ailsa Yates

Amen! This is where it really starts to get good. I hope you felt God embrace you with His hug as you read those words. Meditate on His love and let it soak into your mind and heart. Your heavenly Father will never hurt you or forsake you and His Son, Jesus, has come to be your Savior! He is the Way, the Truth, and the Life! (John 14:6).

So, what is the process of healing? Well, let's first identify where you need healing. If we ask God, He will show us. He is faithful. I have provided some questions to ponder that will help you with this search, but first slowly read your love letter from the Lord! Oh! You're going to love your letters!

Love Letter #1

My Dearest Child,

Grieving is a normal and healthy response to pain. Grieving can cause many other emotions, including denial, anger, and depression. You may have recognized that you are experiencing all, some, or none of these, but one thing remains true—grieving that which needs to be grieved is completely necessary for you to move into acceptance and walk in the freedom and the fruit-filled life I have planned for you. Oh, My sweet child, I will be with you every step of the way. Remember, no one knows you like I do, for I created you: I knit you together in your mother's womb. Therefore, no one knows the depths of your being as I do. I know exactly what you need to grieve and once you trust Me and release this pain once and for all, I will give you a new heart and a new spirit! I will remove your heart of stone and give you a heart of flesh. I promise this in My Word (Ezek. 36:26).

Are you ready to take this journey with Me? I will be your guide. You will begin to understand My plan for your life and how this painful process of grieving fits into that plan. I will take all your painful experiences and turn them into blessings. Listen for My voice; I will help you. Lastly, I have provided someone to walk beside you. This process will allow you to know Me at a deeper level and understand My character more. This is My greatest desire.

Love,

Your Heavenly Father

1. How has your pain changed you?
2. What details do you remember about your painful experience?
3. Can you identify those involved in these painful memories?
4. How have your body, soul, and spirit been affected by your pain?
5. Can you identify any triggers that cause your pain to surface?
6. Can you identify any self-destructive patterns or generational wounds?
7. Describe how you view your identity and worth.
8. How would you describe your wound? What does it look like?

CHAPTER 2

My Story of Healing:
Shattered into Beautiful

Blessed is she who has believed that the Lord
would fulfill his promises to her!
—LUKE 1:45 NIV

I feel it's important before we go any further to share with you my healing story. You need something to cling to and a vision of where you are going. We are told in the Bible, Proverbs 29:18, that without vision people will perish. So, in this section I will focus on the glorious healing the Lord bestowed upon me. If you have experienced abortion, I recommend reading my testimonial book, *Shattered into Beautiful*, in its entirety at a later time.

My story truly is "the woman at the well" story. There were things that caused me to be broken prior to my abortion, but abortion was definitely, as my husband would say, the eye of the storm.

I really did not know what I was doing when I chose abortion. I was lied to by the world and the abortion clinic and told, "It's not a baby yet. It's just tissue." After my abortion, I was in anguish I couldn't explain. All I knew was that something had just happened that should have never happened, and I couldn't go back and change it. I cried until I made myself sick. Rocking back and forth, I thought, "Why didn't anyone ever tell me I would feel this way?" From then on, moment by moment, day by day, my life began to derail. Oh, I tried to fight my guilt, justify my actions, and carry on, but I was haunted by that choice.

First in my efforts to cover up my wound were self-destruction patterns—alcohol, drugs, unhealthy relationships with males. Then depression set in and I battled this for years. Through my sorrow, I stumbled across a Bible my grandmother had given me years ago, and I began to read. It was then, all alone, that Jesus tugged at my heart and I accepted Him as my Savior. I was desperate to know and feel real love. Afterwards, things began to change. I knew God had forgiven me, but I was still hurting form the abortion.

I soon met my husband and we were married. My husband had never played a part in an abortion, but he soon came to realize the impact it had on me. Neither of us knew what to do and it was devastating our marriage. The depression got worse when I tried to have a baby and couldn't get pregnant. At times, I had suicidal thoughts. The enemy would whisper lies to me and I believed them. I still did not realize the source of the depression was my abortion, but in fact it was. As a result of all of it, I lost my vision to any bright future. My husband realized I was in trouble, began to pray, and God victoriously answered his prayers.

The prayer was answered through discovery of a crisis pregnancy center listed in a church bulletin. My husband thought it could help me with my pain and encouraged me to call them. So, I did, and that phone call changed my life. I was invited to participate in a post-abortion Bible study, which I did. It was through that study I experienced my "woman at the well" story—my encounter with Jesus.

I was asked to express a word that reflected the pain in my life. The word "shattered" immediately came to me and I envisioned a piece of shattered glass. God later told me He was going to bring beauty from every painful thing I had experienced. I believed Him from the depths of my heart.

God was urging me to trust Him. In order to fully trust Him with the deep pain of my abortion, I needed to understand His character. I began to study the names of God. As God revealed Himself through these names, I became more familiar with His nature. I had heard these names before, but this time I experienced them on a more intimate level, intimate because He was personally meeting my needs through His names.

> *As I called on His name, He cured me—restoring me emotionally, spiritually, and physically.*

I tried to narrow down one name to claim for my life. They were all so good. As I prayed, God revealed to me that His names meet specific needs. God directed me to the name Jehovah-Rapha, which means, "The Lord My Healer." I am tearful as I can recall the very moment He spoke to my heart and said, "Jeannie, I have come for you. I am yours. I am your Healer."

For me, there is no sweeter name than Jehovah-Rapha. As I called on His name, He cured me—restoring me emotionally, spiritually, and physically.

I realized during the study how bitter my heart was. I asked God to turn my bitterness into sweetness. I asked Him, "Please, Lord, show me what to do to be healed." I had spent years running away from the memory and sin of my abortion. Why was I running? I was wearing myself out from running but getting nowhere. God was there with me when I had the abortion. He heard everything. He saw everything. There was no reason to run. He patiently waited until I stopped, turned around, and faced my problem. The moment I did, He was waiting with open arms to be my liberator.

I no longer had to hide anything. He knew my pain. He knew the deep, dark, shameful secrets of my heart (see Psalm 44:21). The God of the universe who created me still loved me regardless of my sin and He brought me comfort. I had not given God enough credit. When He said He was my Healer, He meant He was my Healer and it was time for me to respond. I started truly accepting God as my personal Savior. The knowledge I was gaining from the study was preparing me to receive His healing and apply it to my life.

No one knew of my participation in the study except for my mom, my husband, Carter, and one dear friend. Carter and my friend encouraged me along, but Mom felt that continuing the study would be difficult for me. She didn't feel I needed to relive all the pain from my abortion. Her motherly instinct was to protect her child, and although I love her dearly for it, she couldn't have been more wrong. Reliving that pain was exactly what needed to happen.

I had to overcome my years of denial. What was I trying to hide by choosing abortion? I believe I was trying to hide my sin of having premarital sex. I sinned to cover up another sin. I was just hurting myself. Right? Wrong. I was hurting myself and God. He was the one against whom I was sinning.

I realized my sexual impurities. I read 1 Corinthians 6:15 (KJV) and was immediately convicted. This Scripture may sound harsh, but sometimes the truth of God's Word is harsh. It reads, "Do you not know that your bodies are members of Christ? Shall I then take members of Christ, and make them the members of a harlot? God forbid." My body was God's temple and I had dishonored it.

God brought to mind each and every sexual sin I had committed. I had been forgiven of these sins, but now it was important to heal from them. I asked God to purify me from my sexual sin. This was not an instant process, as God revealed every sexual memory from all my previous relationships. Individually, I recalled the sin and asked God to purify me from my sexual immorality.

Then I had to face the fact I had ended my unborn baby's life. This was the most difficult stage of my recovery, but it was necessary in order for me to accept the reality of my loss. Scripture showed me that the world had lied to me. My baby was not a mass of tissue. It was indeed a life that began at conception. Psalm 139:15–17 says that God creates every life from its earliest days in the womb. The earliest days are conception. God alone originates life (see Genesis 1:26–27).

In Jeremiah 1:5 (NKJV), God says, "Before I formed you in the belly I knew you." God clearly makes the statement that He alone knits every life together and knows us even before we come forth from the womb. This strongly destroys the discussion of life beginning after exiting the womb.

As I recognized my baby's life, I began to grieve tremendously. The facilitators from the Bible study had given us a copy of a human embryology chart to take home and review. As I did, God began revealing details to me. I was able to remember that it was cold outside when I had my abortion, so I determined it must have been in the late fall or winter months. The only other thing I had remembered was how far along I was in my pregnancy, which was about eight weeks.

That night as I studied the embryology of my baby, I was severely emotionally broken. The pain I endured was greater than the abortion itself. I learned that at eight weeks my baby could respond to touch and could feel pain. At eight weeks the organs and body systems are present. I was in agony, to say the least, knowing my baby could feel pain. My eyes locked on those words, and I began weeping like a child. I was crying so loudly my husband came into the room. He found me lying on the floor wrapped in a blanket. The tears were coming so fast I was having difficulty getting my breath.

He scooped me up and said, "Jeannie, what is wrong?"

I showed him the handout and said to him, "What kind of woman am I? I took the life of my baby. I hurt my baby! Oh, God! My baby could feel the pain." As I continued to cry, I was devastated to know my baby felt the pain of being ripped out of my womb. As he held me I began praying out to God. "Oh God, please, please, I pray you spared my baby from feeling any pain."

I continued to pray this over and over, rocking back and forth just as I had on the day of my abortion. I was seeking comfort. This was a very dramatic scene. The episode almost caused me to stop the study. I told my husband I couldn't continue. I couldn't bear it. He encouraged me to stick with the study and see it through. He said, "I know God has a plan and a purpose for your life." He asked me to call one of my facilitators and share my struggles with her. I agreed to do so.

As I talked to my facilitator, she explained to me that this sorrow must take place in order for me to receive God's healing. She prayed with me and encouraged me, saying that once this journey was complete, I would be a new creation in Christ. Because she had walked a similar path, I believed her. Her beauty always lit up the room. I knew she was filled with joy, and I wanted what she had. I made the commitment to continue no matter how hard it got.

My husband helped carry my burden through this process. He too was committed to this recovery period. My pain had affected him and our marriage. At this point in the recovery, here is what he was able to write in his journal:

> God has answered my prayers. Jeannie has been going through a Bible study for post-abortion women. The lessons are difficult for Jeannie due to the emotional content. She wanted to quit after the first few meetings. She stated she could not handle the memories of what happened. I encouraged her to continue. I know God is at work. Lately she has seemed emotionally worse than before she started. She walks around in a bewildered state after the meetings, upset about the knowledge she is gaining. Sometimes she goes to bed early, crying herself to sleep. I want to rescue her, but I must step back and let God work. I know a lot of walls have to be broken down in order to build back a strong, happy, beautiful woman.

It was true. I did not need Carter to rescue me. I needed God to rescue me.

As I drew close to God, I could feel His presence with me. Sometimes His presence was so strong and alive I felt I could reach out and touch Him. It was as though He was sitting right across the room. He began to speak to me through Scripture. When God shows me Scripture, I always date it in my Bible. Sometimes He will bring my attention back to the same Scripture and I will date it again. When this happens, I pay close attention because I believe He is trying to tell me something.

On three different occasions He guided me to Exodus 19:5–6. It reads:

> Now therefore, if you will obey my voice indeed, and keep my covenant, then you will be a peculiar [special]

treasure unto me above all people: for all the earth is mine and you shall be unto me a kingdom of priests, and an holy nation. These are the words which you shall speak unto the children of Israel. (KJV)

I didn't know what God was trying to say to me, other than that He wanted me to obey. So, I prayed and told God I would be obedient to whatever He called me to do.

As the lessons continued, I juggled everything else in my life. I still struggled with difficulties in conceiving and stayed in prayer about a child. My desire for a child was sometimes more than I could bear. Over the last year my husband and I had become emotionally drained from fertility treatments. Our doctors came to the conclusion there was no reason the two of us could not conceive. It just was not happening. They diagnosed me with "unknown infertility" and encouraged us to explore other fertility options. As heartbreaking as it was, I knew God was not ready to give us our reward. I refused to continue with the fertility treatments and chose to wait on God. I felt I needed to put all my focus and energy into the study in order to fully receive my healing. It was not easy to let go of something I desperately wanted, but I trusted God's timing. I wanted to receive my blessing from Him and Him alone.

Once I came to grips with the fact that my unborn baby was indeed a living being, I asked God to make that truth more real for me. I asked God to give me more insight. I wanted to know if the baby was a boy or girl. I also asked Him to give me a name for him or her. I continued to try to remember more details from my abortion, but I lived so many years in denial and buried the memory so deep, the details were difficult to uncover.

My emotions were overflowing more at home. As much as I tried to hide them, I could see my step-children were concerned.

One day as I was reading my Bible, God laid it heavily on my heart that I should share my story with the children. I said, "God, they are just children. This is too much for them to understand." But honestly, what I feared more was destroying their image of me as their godly stepmother who had brought them to Christ. I was their role model. What would they think of me if they knew I had chosen abortion? I could not ignore God, so I submitted what I thought I heard back to Him. Then I heard, "You said you would obey. Do you not trust Me? Will you not obey Me now?"

Reluctantly, I got up and slowly walked into the room where the children were and shared my story. I explained my abortion and how God had brought me to this study to receive healing. I apologized for my behavior but told them it was necessary for me to recover from my pain. I sat trembling, waiting for their response. Suddenly, they both circled their arms around me and we all cried. No words from them were needed because I could see their hearts through their eyes. It was amazing. God had prepared them to hear from me. I now had the support of not only my husband, but also my family. I had made the mistake of doubting God.

In the next lesson, God began showing me that I was full of anger. I never would have guessed this was an issue for me, but indeed it was. I did not know it was there—it was hidden and denied. As I searched the core of this bitterness, I discovered I was bitter with myself, but also with Mom. I was angry with her for not stopping me from having the abortion. I was angry with her for not discussing it more with me. I was angry because I felt alone in my decision. Untreated anger had remained silent and caused bitterness to root in my heart.

Keep in mind that I did not realize the bitterness was there, so my relationship with my mom carried on as usual through the years. It was not until I began going through the healing process that Mom and I were able to talk about the abortion and I was able to share with her my feelings. I discovered the abortion had caused just as much pain to my mom as it did me, and she also carried regrets. After sixteen years, the two of us were finally able to talk about my abortion. That in itself was healing.

As we talked, Mom remembered something I did not. She told me my baby was due around my birthday, which was in August. This meant I got pregnant around November. Eight weeks later, when I had the abortion, would be sometime in January, which made sense because I remembered the coldness outside. I was excited that I was gaining knowledge. I wanted every single detail to resurface. I felt this was the only way I could heal completely. I took a step further and called the clinic that performed my abortion to request a copy of my medical records.

I told my facilitator about the request for the records. She was shocked and told me she had never had an attendee do this. She encouraged me not to open the findings until the study was over. She felt it was vital to focus on the process of healing. I agreed this was the best thing. Shortly after, the records arrived. I stared at them in my hands. The return address made me cringe. As much as I wanted to open them, I kept my promise and placed them in a safe place until I was ready. I needed to continue my recovery.

I learned through an exercise provided by the study that I needed to forgive my mom, the father of the baby, my friends who were involved, the doctor, and the clinic. I had to let go and forgive all of them. It seemed like too big a mountain to climb, but really it was not. It was very simple. God forgave me and had mercy on me (see Psalm 86:5), therefore forgiveness was not an option. I too had to forgive. I was in no position not to forgive others.

The most difficult person to forgive was myself, at least that's what I thought. However, during this time, I discovered something that freed me. I didn't have or need the power to forgive myself. Forgiveness was a gift already purchased for me. All I had to do was accept it! If I could forgive myself then it wasn't necessary for Christ to die for me. I would be denying God's character and the truth of His Word. This was a huge discovery and one I share frequently today that instantly frees women when they can grasp it. We will talk more about this later.

I also needed to ask forgiveness for the pain I may have caused others, such as the baby's father. That did not require me to contact him. It was between me and God. I had to trust God to take care of the rest. The result of forgiveness brought me much peace. It was important to take care of this issue because unforgiveness hinders prayers (see 1 Peter 3:9–12), and I had much I wanted to ask God for.

Even though I had made much progress, I had to be careful not to let bitterness creep back in. I needed to stay on guard against Satan's attacks and be spiritually prepared for battle. One way I did this was by memorizing Scripture, which also helped me fight depression. I encourage you to pick a Scripture that addresses your struggle. Memorize a verse that will enable you to defeat Satan's attack when it arises. Notice, I did not say if, I said when. The Bible clearly tells us that trouble will come to all of us.

Satan continually used my desire for a child to try to reinstate my depression. Because of all my other obstacles, depression was the hardest stage for me to overcome. It came and went. My depression was born when I took my grief, anger, and unforgiveness, and turned them inward. The depression was self-inflicted, but I was able to overcome it by changing my thought process. When I felt negativity trying to take over, I tried to focus on all the positive things with which God had blessed me. If the attack was stronger than I was, I cried out to God in my trouble and He saved me from distress (see Psalm 107:13). The Bible says God will bring you out of darkness and break your chains apart (see Psalm 107:14). God was doing just that. But I wanted to be fully delivered, so I pleaded with God for complete release.

By now I was more than halfway through the study. I waited for my full deliverance to come. I was going away for a couple days to attend a conference for work. I was excited because all expenses were paid and my husband was going with me. At the last minute, my husband's schedule changed, preventing him from going. I was sad because I really wanted to spend some time with him. But as it turned out, God had other plans. He wanted me to spend time with Him and not my husband.

Once I checked into my hotel room and got settled in, I pulled out my Bible. I worked on some homework from my Bible study class. The peace and quiet was wonderful. I felt God's presence very strongly. I missed my husband, but I knew if he had been there the two of us would be out sightseeing, which meant I would not be in my room working on my study. Then I realized this trip was a gift from God. He had arranged it so the two of us would be absolutely alone. I thought, "What is God doing?" There had to be a purpose. As I meditated on this truth, I felt extremely special. I looked around the beautiful room given to me for my pleasure. Everything was perfect! For the first time since I pranced around the floor in my little girl pumps, I felt like a princess.

The next morning, I went to class. I was thankful for the knowledge I was gaining to enhance my profession, but I was eager to return to my room and dive back into my studies. Finally, 5:00 P.M. came and I headed back to my little paradise. Hunger struck. No problem, I thought, as I had been given a very generous food allowance. I scanned the room service menu. The meals looked exquisite. I was getting ready to order dinner when suddenly I felt God wooing me. I didn't want to miss a second with Him. The food could wait. His words are more necessary than food (see Job 23:12). I dropped the menu and went over to my Bible.

I wasn't sure what God wanted me to see, so I got face down on the floor and started praying. I know what you must be thinking. Face down on a hotel floor. Yuck! But this is the posture I take when I am seeking God. He is pleased when we humble ourselves before Him. Don't misunderstand me. I am not saying you need to get on your face during your prayer time. You can come to God in any posture with a humble heart. This posture is what I personally choose to use.

Once I stopped praying, I sat up and reached for my Bible and notes from the study. I came across a Scripture I had circled. Obviously, it was a Scripture one of the facilitators had given me, but I did not remember the content so I looked it up. I turned the pages with an eager and expectant heart. Finally, I reached Ezekiel 36:25. That night, sixteen years after my abortion, God said to me, "I will sprinkle clean water upon you, and you shall be clean" (KJV). Tears started pouring from my eyes, but they felt as if they were pouring from my heart. I stared at the verse for a long time until God urged me to read on. There was more.

Still sitting on the floor, I read Ezekiel 36:26: "A new heart also will I give you, and a new spirit will I put within you: and I will take away the stony heart out of your flesh, and give you an heart of flesh" (KJV). Something was happening. It was though my heart was being stripped—as if it was being torn down and rebuilt. I was weeping. I placed the Scriptures across my heart and lay back on the floor and allowed God to perform His miracle. "And God shall wipe away all tears from their eyes and there shall be no more death, neither sorrow, nor crying, neither shall

there be any more pain for the former things have passed away"
(Rev. 21:4 KJV).

It was that night when God took something shattered and
turned it into something beautiful. I am so glad I was obedient
to what He wanted me to do because it was in that moment of
obedience that God completely deliv-
ered me and healed me from my abortion pain. He knew the words I needed
to hear from Him and He knew when
I would be ready to receive them. Your
words may be different. What makes
the experience so supernatural is that when God meets your
personal needs, He becomes your personal Savior.

*When God meets
your personal needs,
He becomes your
personal Savior.*

I am not sure how long I lay there, but when I finally got up,
I knew I was a new woman . . . and I was starved. Feeling light
as a feather, I pranced over and picked up the menu to order my
dinner. After placing my order, I soaked in God's presence until
there was a knock on the door.

"Room service." I opened the door to find a sparkling silver
tray.

"Thank you," I said. I carried it to the table and unveiled my
requested dinner of:

Rosemary Roasted Moroccan Lamb
Olive Oil Glazed Potatoes
Steamed Asparagus
Warm Roll with Butter
Spinach Salad with Cranberry Red Wine Sauce
Rum Raisin Bread Pudding with Pecan Caramel Sauce
Water and Sweet Tea

The meal was served on the most elegant, beautiful china. It was so good. I ate until my belly hurt. It was the most expensive meal I had ever had. I stayed awake as long as I could. I didn't want the night to end. I wanted it to last forever. When my eyelids wouldn't stay open any longer, I crawled into bed.

The next morning, I got up refreshed and packed my suitcase. It was time to go home. As I made my way to the door, my heart was sad to leave such a special place. I turned around to take one more look at my little paradise, when God spoke to my heart and said, "My child, be uplifted. Your new heart leaves with you and so do I."

Once I got home, I shared with my husband what had happened. We both rejoiced in answered prayer.

The next day I returned to work. My supervisor asked, "Did you have a good time, Jeannie?"

"The best," I replied as I placed my expenses on her desk and quickly exited the room. I am sure she was taken aback when she reviewed my meal receipt totaling seventy-five dollars. Ouch! A meal not only fit for a princess, but fit for a queen.

Now, I want to share something very personal with you. One of the most profound things I experienced as I healed from my abortion was the opportunity to seek God in knowing if my baby was a boy or a girl. He answered me and told me it was a girl. As I sought further, God gave me a name for her, Abagail, which means the Father's Joy.

You see, names are significant. God even reveals Himself through His names. One of the privileges we have as parents is to name our children. If my baby had been born, I would have named her. Through God's mercy and love, He was now giving me the opportunity. He was now giving me her name, but it didn't stop there.

The greatest gift was the acceptance I was able to capture as I marveled at the life of my Abagail. This was essential to my healing. I acknowledged before man and God that my aborted baby was indeed real—a beautiful gift from above. With the support of my husband and children, we publicly memorialized her death. This gave me the chance to celebrate her life. She was worthy and this was essential to the grieving process. One of the most difficult, but necessary things for post-abortion women is that through their suffering they are afforded the opportunity to grieve and honor their babies. This is vital to their healing.

If you have suffered from an abortion, I encourage you to sit down with God and begin to pray, just as I did. Ask Him to speak to you about your baby. Discover the gift He has for you. Plan a special way to honor the life of your child.

One morning I decided to sit down and write Abagail a letter. This was not an attempt to communicate with her. Scripture is very clear that communication with the dead is prohibited. This was simply a way to express my feelings on paper. In a moment of silence, I began to write what my heart was longing to say to her.

Dear Abagail,

You and I were taken away from each other so long ago. It was such a confusing and lonely time. There were so many wounds in my life. Even before you, I was searching for ways to ease the pain of those wounds. I was so young with no guidance and next thing I knew there you were. Your presence made me more confused and scared, and I felt like I had nowhere to turn. I made a wrong choice to let you go.

I want to say to you that I am so sorry, my sweet one. On that cold winter day Mommy did not know what she was doing. For so long I have hurt and carried the burden of our bond being broken. I have imagined your beauty and wondered how you are. You will soon be sixteen and, oh, how I have missed you through the years. Somehow, I know if you could, you would let me know you miss me too and you are doing fine.

I dropped the pen. As the Spirit prompted me, I closed my eyes, peace filled my soul, and a reply came, which was inspired by the Holy Spirit.

Mom, you don't have to worry, be sad, or wonder if I hurt because on that cold day you made a wrong choice, God was there. He took my tiny little hand and led me safely home. There is no pain here, no tears, so, Mom, it is okay. You have been forgiven and I will see you soon.

I know my leaving left such a void in your life, but God wants you to fill it with joys. Share our story and use it to save others like me. For those like you, teach them. Teach them as God taught you not to be burdened with sorrow, but to lift up your heart to Him and trade it for peace and the sunshine of tomorrow.

I wrote what I heard and, lastly, I promised Abagail I would bring purpose to her life. I then wrote a letter of thanks to God and placed them both in a beautiful keepsake box which is displayed in our home. Abagail is a part of our family and we openly celebrate her life. This has brought so much healing.

If you are reading this and you have experienced an abortion, I want you to know there is a lasting healing available for you. Abortion destroys, emotionally, physically, and spiritually. As post-abortive women, it is hard to talk about the circumstances surrounding our choice and the experience itself. So, we don't, and we are left to carry a heavy burden. Sweet friend, God wants to heal you. He wants you to know that you have carried the heavy burden of this secret far too long and it's time to let it go!

Reach out to your local pregnancy crisis center. Many of them provide abortion recovery assistance. If your local center does not, reach out to me. I will help you locate some help. You are one courageous step away from getting your miracle!

In the meantime, know this—nothing can separate you from the love of God, not even abortion. Mercy triumphs over judgment (Jas. 2:13).

CHAPTER 3

Power in the Name

We will sing for joy over your victory, and
in the name of our God we will set up our
banners.

—PSALM 20:5 NASB

C an we trust God with our pain? The answer is yes! Most women find it difficult to approach God with their pain. Through my years of counseling, I have discovered three possible reasons why one may find it difficult to approach God with the pain in their past. First, they may have an unbelieving heart. Second, their pain has caused the heart to grow calloused, and third, they may have a misconception about the character of God. For example, after my abortion, I attempted to bury my grief, turn off my emotions, and move on. I kept myself busy. I was always running. Running from what? My past, the memories, maybe God. I believed in God, but my pain was so great, I had an unbelieving heart that He could or wanted to do anything about it. Most days I felt all alone, trying to hide my shame, but God was there always desiring to reveal Himself. I clearly did not know God's nature.

You see, I was raised in church, and even though I had memorized all the books of the Bible, I lacked the true meaning of Christianity. I thought it was a list of things I could or couldn't do. I didn't know how to have a personal and intimate relationship with Christ or how to follow Him. So, eventually, church became something I was expected to do, not something I wanted to do. Boy! Did I have it all wrong. It wasn't until years later that I would discover the truth, which is that God did not call us to religion, but to an intimate relationship with His Son, Jesus! Religion condemns us; Jesus forgives us. Religion confines us; Jesus sets us free. Religion hurts us; Jesus heals us. Religion makes us feel like we will never measure up; Jesus says we are blameless in His sight.

Religion has caused us to run away, instead of running towards the one who chose us and loves us. "Because of his great love for us, God who is rich in mercy, made us alive with Christ even when we were dead in transgressions—it is by grace we have been saved and God raised us up with Christ and seated us with him in the heavenly realms in Christ Jesus" (Eph. 2:4–6 NIV).

Oh, sweet friend, take a moment and let this sink in. In His fullness, we have received grace upon grace. The world, the enemy, even our flesh will condemn us, but Jesus came into the world not to condemn us, but to SAVE us! (John 3:17).

God wants us to fully know who He is. He is everything we need Him to be. He is "I AM." I want you to know that at the time of your painful experience, God was there. He grieved with you. It was never God's plan for harm to come to you, but we live in a fallen world. What He does promise is that our present sufferings are not worth comparing the glory that will be revealed in us (Rom. 8:18). He also promises that in all things God works for the good of those who love Him and have been called according to His purpose (Rom. 8:28). This is great news!

So, God is going to take your experience and bring goodness out of it! Done deal!

God is urging you to trust Him. In order to fully trust Him with your deepest pain, you must understand His character. Even though you may have thought less of yourself, God never did. He still looked upon you with love, because this is His character, LOVE. It is a gift! He has seen all our failures and flaws and He still calls us friend, and His beloved child.

No matter how hard we try to hide our brokenness, God's grace will find us and put us back together again. Oh! How I love this promise! He is the master craftsman who weaves us back together again. As I searched Scripture, I discovered that God revealed His names to His people only as they needed them—in moments of deepest crisis. You see, I knew about God, but it wasn't until I found myself in complete brokenness from the pain of my abortion, that I come to really *know* God personally. When He met my personal need, when He reached down and touched me, healed me, He became my personal Savior. This experience totally changed my relationship with Him, but I had to be willing to allow Him to do His perfect work in me. I had to be willing to roll up my sleeves and do a little work to uncover my gifts.

> *No matter how hard we try to hide our brokenness, God's grace will find us and put us back together again.*

God is such a nurturer. The definition of nurture is to give tender care and protection to a child, a young animal, or a plant, helping it to grow and develop. it also means to encourage somebody or something to grow, develop, thrive, and be successful.

What a beautiful description of who God is in our life. A picture of what the daughters of God so desperately need to give and receive. Even in this moment, God is stirring your heart. He is awakening you to His love and His role in your life. He is awakening you to the need you have for Him to nurture you. It is a need that can only be filled by Him.

The truth is, there has never been more of a desperate need for the presence of nurture than it is today. We must be enveloped by His nature if we are going to survive. Our relationship with God is a safe and intimate place. We are indeed heartsick and in need of this intimate and safe place. We are in need of this God of nurture. The world is crying out for Him. Truth and love made simple.

As we move through this section, we will be evaluating the difference between our earthly fathers and our heavenly Father. If our earthly father is absent from our lives we can be left in a very vulnerable position. At the same time, our father could be present and cause extreme pain by his actions, or non-actions. In both cases, this can lead to a false view of fatherhood which ultimately damages our perspective of our heavenly Father, unless we know His character.

This is a good time to share a little more of my personal story. As a child, I often dreamt of a perfect family. Even now, I am reflecting on a memory. I was a young girl returning home from school. Lost in my dream, I stared out the window of the school bus. Suddenly, the bus stopped in front of my house. I was eager to get inside and tell my parents about my day. I ran through the front yard with my backpack swinging from side to side, hoping my parents would meet me at the front door. But this hope was all a fantasy. This perfect family I dreamt of never existed. No one met me at the door—only the evidence of a dysfunctional family. Sin in several forms had found its way into my family's life and caused us to be broken and divided. As a result, my parents divorced when I was at an early age and my dad became absent from my life.

My mom worked hard to provide for her children. Unfortunately, the financial demands of being a single parent caused her career to steal most of her time from us. As a result, we did not spend much time together. For years, I watched other families function and listened to my friends brag about how they were "Daddy's little girl." I didn't understand why my life could not be like theirs. Resentment grew in my heart about the life I had been given.

By age fifteen, I was experiencing the taste of alcohol and enjoying attention from the opposite sex. The attention I was getting seemed to fill a need, and I became hungry for more. I did not know it at the time, but I was trying to replace the male companionship missing from my life that should have been supplied by my dad.

Through counseling I learned that among teenage females, parental divorce and/or absent fathers has been associated with lower self-esteem, sexual activity, delinquent behaviors, and more difficulty establishing a gratifying, lasting relationship with the opposite sex. Unfortunately, I experienced all of these and they continued to bring hardship to my life.

As a female, I needed my father to be involved in my life. My desire to be valued as a daughter seemed to be a key element in developing the confidence that I was indeed loved. I turned my pain inward. I felt I was not pretty enough, athletic enough, or smart enough to be loved.

Studies have shown that many young girls experience an appetite for males if their father is absent. Girls need a father in their lives who is attentive and loving. I once heard fatherhood described as a security blanket. Without this blanket, girls can go astray. They become emotionally dependent on others for the lack of love and the masculine example fathers should have provided.

As I mentor and counsel young girls today, I can almost immediately discern that there is a father absent in their life. They carry brokenness, unworthiness, and many are not interested in a relationship with God. Why? Because by nature, our earthy fathers were created to be an image, an example, of our heavenly Father. So, when that image is distorted, it becomes damaging in our lives, we believe lies, and they push us away from the very one we need to draw close to: God.

So, here are just a few of the lies we began to believe:

- God is just like my father.
- I am not worth loving.
- God cannot meet my needs.
- I must fulfill my own emotional needs.

We battle these lies because our needs were not met by our earthly father and when there is an emotional detachment from the father, we will fill that void with the wrong things and the wrong people, and unfortunately, we know there are many out there that will take advantage of a young woman that is not being shepherded by her daddy.

So, what does a young woman need from her father?

- She needs his involvement.
- She needs a demonstration of a healthy marriage.
- She needs his support.
- She needs his trust.
- She needs his unconditional love.
- She needs a strong spiritual leader.
- She needs a positive role model.

The need of influence from a father is even greater than that of a mother. Fathers appear to have an impact on their daughters which is needed to navigate key events in their early adulthood, such as academic success, relationships, mental health, and overall coping with life. In such a dark and influential culture as ours, and at such young crucial ages, young women need to be fulfilled at home. They need to be covered with their security blanket so they are not tempted to taste the evils of the world. Simply put, girls need their daddies. They need daddies to shepherd and protect them. They need daddies to comfort and love them.

I love my family very much, and I am not in any way trying to put blame on them for my choices. My choices were mine alone. Actually, I thank God for my family because it was all part of His plan to shape me into the woman He desired me to be so I could fulfill my purpose. I share these details only so you, as my readers, have a good understanding of who I was, and the circumstances surrounding me that I believe influenced my choices. I also share this portion of my story because I believe many of you can relate in some fashion.

The truth is I had a difficult time approaching God and trusting Him with my pain, because the only example I had of a father abandoned me and hurt me. Now, let me tell you how good God is. Through the years, God allowed such healing and reconciliation between me and my daddy. Once I experienced the grace of my heavenly Father, I extended it to my earthly father, realizing he never had a father himself. Simply put, he was not able to give me what I needed, because he was lacking it himself. Have you ever researched the childhood history of your parents? Discovering the truth about what my daddy was lacking helped me to release him from all my unmet expectations. The truth was he was a broken vessel, just like me. A sinner in need of a Father; a sinner in need of a Savior.

This viewpoint turned my resentfulness into mercy. My daddy became my dear friend and through our conversations and the love of Christ we both experienced healing. This was a gift to me. I realize some of you may have not been afforded the same opportunity. In this case, understanding the character of God becomes extremely important. We understand the character of God through His names.

So, pause right here. Grab your pen, journal, and Bible. It's time to huddle up and dig in. Let's explore God's nature further, and watch as He turns your painful experience into a blessing. Watch as He shows you how this experience of grieving and suffering fits into His perfect plan!

Behold . . . I will heal them and reveal to them
the abundance of peace and truth.
—JEREMIAH 33:6 (NKJV)

Now, let's look at some biblical examples. But first, go ahead and read your next love letter.

Love Letter #2

My Dearest Child,

I am approachable. You can trust Me with all your hurts. It is important to understand My character. Sometimes My children have a much too small, too cramped, too human view of who I really am. I am the GREAT I AM!! That means I am everything you need Me to be. I do not change. My promise is the same to you today as it was to Moses.

Knowing who I am will encourage you to be like Me, to love Me, and to respond to Me in obedience by bringing your needs to Me. You will be introduced to many of My great names. Seek Me as you review them and I will speak to you and show you which name you need to call Me during this time. Through My name I will meet your needs and reveal My character to you.

I want to be your Father. Are you comforted by that idea or does the word "father" bring feelings of confusion and hurt? If it does, know that I am your heavenly Father. I will meet all the needs that your earthly father failed to or was unable to meet. My love is greater for you. Now child, I need you to approach Me. I need you to surrender your heart and trust Me. Nothing can separate you from My love, NOTHING.

Love,

Your Heavenly Father

All throughout the Bible names have great significance. A name defines the unique nature of that person. Let's consider Abraham, Isaac, and Jacob. Abraham and Jacob had their name changed by God. Isaac did not, because He was named personally by God. In each case, the name change was given during a time of crisis and it influenced that person's character and destiny. Now, we are going to focus on a few of God's names and how He chose to reveal Himself. The same God that revealed Himself then, also does so today. As you study, consider by what name God is now revealing Himself to you.

1. **Jehovah–Jireh (God, My Provider)** is first mentioned in Genesis 22:1–14. Here we discover Abraham taking his son Isaac to Mount Moriah, where he was willing to offer him as a sacrifice to the Lord. When they arrived at the foot of the mountain, something profound happened. Abraham told his servants, "Stay here . . . **we will come back to you**" (22:5 NIV). Abraham had great faith that God would raise his son from the dead. However, God provided in another way (v. 13). What did Abraham's experience reveal about the character of God?

2. What did God do for Abraham?

3. The story has a beautiful ending, and so does yours! What does God promise to provide for you in Isaiah 61:2–3, 7?

Abraham didn't stop and say, "Lord, this is too much for me to handle." Abraham had faith the Lord would provide and give him all power and strength to obey Him. He trusted God would meet all his needs and He did. Two thousand years later, He provided the ultimate sacrifice, His Son, to save us all. Our God sees all our needs and He provides for His people! "He who did not spare His own Son, but delivered Him up for us all, how will He not also with Him freely give us all things?" (Rom. 8:32 NASB).

4. **Jehovah-Rapha (God, My Healer)** I love this one! This name is first found in Exodus 15. Three days after Moses led the people through the Red Sea, God revealed Himself by His name to His people. Who did God tell His people He is in Exodus 15:22–26?

5. Under what conditions would the Israelites be healed? (Exod. 15:26).

God wanted to use the bitter waters as a mirror for their hearts. Bitterness many times rises up in a person who has experienced a deep disappointment with the Lord. Many times it comes from a crisis such as, but not limited to: divorce, financial difficulty, death, abuse, relationship struggles, abandonment, rejection. Can you relate? How?

In Hebrew, "Rapha" or "healer" means "doctor" or "physician." "Jesus answered and said to them, 'Those who are well have no need of a physician, but those who are sick. I have not come to call the righteous, but sinners, to repentance'" (Luke 5:31 NKJV).

Let's take a close look at Isaiah 53:4–5 (KJV) and the promises of healing contained there. Put your name in each blank.

"Surely he has borne _____ griefs and carried _____ sorrows. Yet we esteemed him stricken. Smitten by God, and afflicted, but he was wounded for _____ transgressions. He was bruised for_____ iniquities. The chastisement for _____ peace was upon him and by his stripes _____ is healed."

God Himself chose, made a decision, to be the healer of His people. What is the requirement for healing? Simply to listen to the voice of God (Exod. 15:26) and believe in grace that Jesus was the final fulfillment of the healing covenant of God for His people. That's right! It's finished and available for all! This provision was not just for the spiritual realm, but for the physical as well.

Anyone need a doctor? "... For I am the Lord who heals you" (Exod. 15:26 NKJV).

6. In Genesis 16:1-16, we are introduced to **El Roi (The God Who Sees)** and a woman named Hagar. We are going to talk more about Hagar in the next chapter, but for now, can you relate to her story?

7. What or whom have you run away from?

8. What promises does God give when you feel alone, rejected, abandoned? (Note that these feelings can lead to insecurity and fear.)

    1 Peter 2:4

    Philippians 4:19

    Psalm 27:10

    Deuteronomy 31:6

9. **Jehovah-Shalom (God, My Peace)** The story of Gideon is found in Judges 6. The angel of the Lord appeared to Gideon and told him that he would be a mighty man of valor (v. 12). It was believed that if you saw an angel of the Lord you might not survive, so Gideon thought his time had come to an end. But the Lord spoke, "Peace to you, do not fear; you shall not die." Read Judges 6:17–23.

10. The Hebrew word for "peace" is shalom. In Israel, you will be greeted by everyone with the word "shalom." Read Judges 6:24. What is the name of the altar Gideon built unto the Lord?

11. We can have peace even in difficult circumstances. Where does our peace come from?

    John 14:27

John 16:33

12. **Jehovah-Rohe (God, My Shepherd)** Read Psalm 23. Notice the personal relationship between us and our Shepherd. "I shall not want" is quite comforting. Name all the things He promises to give you in this psalm, verse by verse.

13. Our Great Shepherd is with us no matter what we are going through. He will take our side and stand as our Banner. Our banner is in the name of our Lord, our Shepherd, and His victory becomes our victory as we set up our banners in His name. Where does He say we will dwell and for how long? (Psa. 23:6).

14. **Jehovah-Shammah (God Is There)** Read Ezekiel 48:35. God is there and knows everything. What is one way you can respond? (Psa. 32:5).

15. The last nine chapters of Ezekiel are connected to the restoration of Israel and rebuilding the city and temple. How might God be rebuilding and restoring you right now? Read Jeremiah 33:6–9.

God wants us to know Him as a faithful Father. One that is always there, always in our heart, and in the midst of our lives in all circumstances.

16. To whom will God be a Father? (Psa. 68:5).

17. God is our heavenly Father, but in many ways He is both mother and father to us. Read the following verses.

    Deuteronomy 1:31
    Isaiah 49:15
    Matthew 7:11

God is the perfect parent. How can we learn to release our earthly parents from any unmet expectations?

18. In what parental role does God reveal Himself in Isaiah 66:13?
19. What are some ways a mother comforts a child?
20. Can you imagine God comforting you this way?
21. What three specific ways that God will comfort you do your find in Zephaniah 3:17?
22. Is there anything still holding you back from trusting God with your pain?
23. What is the difference between discipline and punishment?
24. Have you ever felt punished by God?

Individuals can be tricked to believe God is "punishing" them because of the consequences of their own actions which they may be experiencing. They have fear and lack of trust in their heavenly Father. What they may not understand is that their punishment was placed on the spotless, perfect Lamb, Jesus Christ. On the cross, it was finished! We must not deny what Jesus gave us, but accept it as a gift! On the cross, justice and the love of God meet and seal us into our true identity!

God does not punish us; He disciplines us. Discipline is simply God, through His love, training us and correcting us to reflect His image. Through discipline, He strengthens us, corrects us, and teaches us. He encourages us, blesses us, in the instruction of His Word. He wants the best for us, just as we do for our children. It is why we discipline our own children. Discipline may not always be pleasant, but the outcome will mold us into something beautiful. God is more concerned with our heart and character than our comfort when correction needs to be applied.

25. What does Hebrews 12:10–11 say?
26. **Jehovah-Tsidkenu (God, My Righteousness)** How does God reveal Himself in Jeremiah 23:5–6?

Jeremiah 33:15–16

27. We cannot obtain righteousness through our own efforts, but through faith. What does Paul say in Philippians 3:8–9?
28. Through faith and the work on the cross we have a restored relationship with God. What do the following passages declare?

Hosea 2:19–20

Isaiah 62:4

This begins to show us a beautiful picture! God delights in you! When you unite with Him and take His name, you are clothed with His righteousness. We are identified with Him. We no longer have to be dependent on our own efforts, but rather rest in who we are in Him and allow Him to work through us for His pleasure, His glory, and to be lights in the world. This is good news! We bear His name. We are no longer held back by our sins and failures. Hallelujah!

After reading this chapter, will you trust and approach God with your pain? If not, go back and soak some more. It is vital to accept and believe in the goodness of God and understand His character before moving forward. So, take as much time as you need.

P.S. If I did not list "who" you personally need God to be, take some time to search more of His names. He has many more!

I will close this chapter out with this beautiful quote below. It is so true. We are never alone.

Wherever we go, God is there...
Whenever we call, God is listening...
Whatever we need, God is enough...
— BENNIE EUGENE SCOTT

CHAPTER 4

The Escape

There is nothing concealed that will not
be disclosed, or hidden that will not
be made known.
—LUKE 12:2 NIV

I was determined to do whatever I needed to do to bury any memories connected to my experience and escape. I moved, and moved again, this time to another city, but the memories followed me. I trained my thoughts to deny that the trauma had even taken place and for years that worked, minimally, but the details always seemed to surface.

Denial is one of the most common emotional reactions, especially to any form of trauma or loss. Depending on the circumstances there may be some initial relief, but it won't last. Denial is a way we cope and basically it speaks to "I can't believe I did this," or "I can't believe I allowed this," or "I can't believe this happened." So you choose to believe a deception and deny your reality. It's important to know that denial will run its course just as the other stages of grief will. It is normal. What is important is that we learn how to allow and move through these emotions and stages in a healthy way and not let them manipulate us or trap us. Let's look at a couple of biblical examples.

There are many times when God will direct us to "go back"— to go back and deal with the pain and circumstances so we can ultimately be free. God has given us a biblical example in the story of Hagar. In Genesis chapter 16, we see a picture of Hagar being mistreated and dealt with harshly. In her suffering she ran away. As she was running away, she stopped at a spring in the desert where an angel of the Lord appeared to her and said "Hagar, where have you come from and where are you going?" In which Hagar replied, "I am running away." The angel of the Lord told her to go back! And out of the obedience of going back there would be increase. In verse 11, the angel of the Lord went on to say, "The Lord has heard your misery." Hagar gave a name to the Lord who spoke to her: "You are the God who sees me." For she said, "I have now seen the one who sees me"—El Roi, the God who sees! God was directing Hagar to go back and face the past, ONLY to recover from it. Only to bring increase, blessing.

> *There is nothing concealed that*
> *will not be disclosed, or hidden that*
> *will not be made known.*
> —LUKE 12:2 NIV

I personally had to return back to my past, as hard as it was, and allow God access to the deep places of my heart and the per-mission to do His healing work in me. This would require taking responsibility for my wrong in the situation if there was any and extending forgiveness to others that caused the pain. Now, there are also circumstances where you may have not been at fault at all—you were a total victim. For example, sexual assault and abuse is a horrible trauma to live through. You live in fear and confinement. It's a dark painful place and you may wander what you ever did to deserve it. Well let me answer that question for you. Nothing! You did nothing to deserve it and it does not define who you are! It is horrific violence that you should have never suffered. And let me just pause here for a moment and remind you that vengeance is the Lord's, and He will have it. It is not your fault and our God will redeem all wrong and make it right. He will provide what you need to overcome, but you have to reach out and accept it.

In any case, in the journey back you will discover the greatest freedom and healing. So don't listen to someone who tells you that you don't need to go back and deal with a painful past. Friend, it is exactly what you need to do. But listen, it is very important that you can't go alone! You cannot do this work on your own. You must go with someone who can guide you, and help you, to discover the healing balm of Jesus. You just have to say yes! Trust and obey. Jesus will do the work and provide community for you. Community brings healing, and out of the ashes, I promise you will find beauty.

Through the process, our thoughts have to remain positive, not negative. It is powerful what the mind can do to protect the vessel. We can actually train our thoughts to deny that the trauma, pain, or whatever it is we have encountered ever took place. For a while, that may work minimally, but the details and memories always seem to surface. God brings them to the surface, because they need to be dealt with. He wants to heal you.

Once I was counseling a woman who had come to me needing help healing from a past abortion. After several sessions of healing, she spoke out one day and said that God revealed to her that she had two abortions, not one. She was blown away at how she had put this second abortion in such a deep place of denial that she had actually forgotten she had even had it.

Again–

There is nothing concealed that
will not be disclosed, or hidden that
will not be made known.
—LUKE 12:2 NIV

So, let's talk about our thoughts. Positive thoughts align with Jesus. Negative thoughts align with the enemy. So, feed the mind positive thoughts. Be around positive people that want to see you succeed, that speak positive things over you, and desire to see you fulfill your purpose.

This is why the Bible says to be transformed by the renewing of your mind (Rom. 12:2). Words are very powerful. Think about it: your very salvation depends on your words. You had to confess with your mouth; it was your words that determined eternity for you. So, words have power over us. They define us, they navigate us, and they direct us. So, make sure Jesus' words are defining you, not Satan. Let me explain this further:

Every sin in this world started with a lie, a word spoken, a whisper spoken, a lie.

When we hear the lie, we begin to process it. It becomes vital input that enters the brain.

Then we consider it. We ponder it and it begins to be fertilized and watered.

Then we believe it. It takes root and grows. Deception has occurred.

Then we act upon it. The belief has now turned into action.

As a result, there is bad fruit instead of good fruit and truth, which is what God purposed for us. So, we have to be very careful what we speak and listen to and who we listen to. We have to listen to King Jesus, not the enemy. His Word is truth; everything else is a lie.

John 8:44 tells us he was a murderer from the beginning, not holding to the truth, for there is no truth in him. When he lies, he speaks his native language, for he is a liar and the father of lies!

It is why as parents we have to be careful what we speak over our children. For example: If we say, "You're lazy," they will believe it and any drive to do anything will diminish. It is more effective to speak in a positive way versus the negative, to speak what you want to see achieved. For example: "I know God has given you a spirit of determination to accomplish everything He has called you to and I thank Him for it! No, you are not a messy child. You are a very well organized little being." They will believe what you speak, because of the natural influence you have over them.

It's important to note that God is a good God. It was not His plan for bad things to happen to us. We live in a fallen, sin-filled world. There is going to be suffering. Satan, the enemy, is prowling around constantly, trying to kill, steal, and destroy (John 10:10), but Jesus came that we could have life abundantly! That's how the Scripture ends and that's how the story ends, if we choose well—if we choose Jesus.

Now, I want to talk to you about triggers that cause us to seek escape. When we have experienced great pain, we may also experience what is known as triggers. A trigger is anything that might cause a person to recall a traumatic experience they have had. Triggers could be songs, words, smells, environments, colors, touch, tangible things. There can also be internal triggers, such as anger, anxiety, feelings of abandonment, loneliness, discouragement, despair, vulnerability, and so much more that can leave a person in mental anguish.

When triggers arise, we may use things to cope. Many times it is addictions or anything else that may ease the pain—but it is only temporary, leaving you wanting more. If these things are not dealt with properly, they will cause a downward spiral, leaving things worse. The only thing, the only person, who can ease and heal the pain is Jesus, but many don't know how to grab hold of His help and apply it to their life.

It's not that we don't want to, but sometimes the depth of pain, sorrow, loss, and failures have damaged our self-worth and we begin to believe the lie that we are not even worthy to receive what Jesus wants to offer us. We feel we can't approach God with our pain. This ultimately leads to great depression, and sadly sometimes death. It was never God's plan for us. We have to acknowledge that there is need for emotional, physical, and spiritual help when we have encountered deep traumatic pain in our life.

The mental anguish, the lies whispered to us, come from Satan, the enemy, the father of lies. Those lies need to be uprooted and replaced by the truth and love of Jesus. Our identity needs to be restored and taken back and given to its rightful owner.

Here are three things to help you when seeking to escape pain:

1. Don't run away from the pain; embrace it and seek help. Take a bold and courageous step.
2. Replace all negative thoughts with positive in every way you can, casting down every lie.
3. Discover your identity by reading the book of Ephesians, particularly chapters 1–3, and highlight or underline every word that defines who you are.

Now, let's look at one more biblical example. The story of Peter is the greatest story of denial we see in the Bible. I personally love his story. I find such raw truth there—someone I can relate to. At the same time, I find such promise and hope. There are others you may relate to, but right now let's take a closer look at our dear friend Peter.

1. How did Peter deny the Lord in Luke 22: 54–62?
2. What kind of pressures was Peter trying to relieve by denial?
3. How did he respond afterwards? (v. 62).

Let this narrative about Peter pour over you. Think about how you can relate in regard to your own story.

Peter's story is real. It's personal. Peter's story is our story. It's a story of grace, love, and renewal. Jesus called Peter in John 1 after Andrew told Simon they had found the Messiah. Jesus saw Simon and renamed him Peter, which means "rock." Simon Peter was called again in Luke 5. There Jesus told him to become a fisher of men. We see that Peter was a risk-taker. He got out of the boat and went walking on the water! Peter also went up the mountain and experienced the great transfiguration. So, Peter experienced many miracles first hand. Peter also had a mouth. One that worked for Jesus, but also against him. Peter said Jesus was the Christ, the Messiah, the one they had all been waiting for. Then on the night Jesus was betrayed Peter opened his mouth again. Peter denied knowing Jesus not once, not twice, but three times! After Peter's denial something changed. Peter's boldness and confidence were shattered. He was more like sand, not like the "rock" that Jesus had named him. His identity had been damaged, stolen. He ran away and wept after his denial, because he knew who and what he was, a sinner in need of for-

Peter's story is our story. It's a story of grace, love, and renewal.

giveness just like you and just like me. At that moment, his entire being depended on Jesus. He had to know for himself if Jesus had really risen from the dead, because then maybe he could be renewed. Maybe there was hope. Maybe Jesus would forgive him. Peter had failed. He knew this all too well. He ran from the crowd that arrested Jesus. He did not stand up and acknowledge his friend and Savior. He denied even knowing Him after walking with Him so closely and witnessing His miracles.

Afterwards, Peter returned to his old ways. He returned to what he knew and trusted. His failures haunted him. He couldn't shake the thought of what he had done. Filled with shame, he returned to what was familiar, the past, to seek out a living doing what he was comfortable with, fishing. He was hard at work all night and caught nothing. This too is familiar. He was even a failure at fishing. It seemed all was lost for Peter. He wondered how he could even carry on. Suddenly, a voice called from across the shore. "Friends, have you caught any fish? Throw your nets on the other side and you will find some." Where had Peter heard this voice before? He picked up the net and tossed it on the other side and what a catch! They couldn't even pull the net in. Then John figured it out. "It's the Lord," he said. That was all Peter needed to know. Erratic, spontaneous Peter was back! He jumped in the water and swam as fast as he could to the shore, but when he got there, he didn't say anything. No conversation is recorded in the book of John. The rest of them arrived and ate breakfast in silence. Maybe Peter found if difficult to approach the one he ran away from, the one he denied, the one he crucified. Peter needed Jesus to reach out to him to heal and forgive him.

Jesus finally turned to Peter and He said, "Simon, son of John, do you truly love Me?" He asked Peter three times. Peter responded, "Yes, Lord, You know I love You. Yes, Lord, You know

I love You. You know all things; You know I love You." Jesus tenderly reached out to this wounded, frightened child. Peter had made the biggest mistake of his life and now he faced the one he denied, the one he rejected. Peter couldn't even talk. He couldn't approach Jesus. Jesus had to come to Peter.

We are no different. When life's biggest mistakes occur, we find it difficult to go to the one we offended, or who offended us, or to embrace a great struggle we may be facing. We are more likely to stay in hiding and tuck our sorrow or mistake deep down where no one can find it, to deny it, and carry on.

However, Jesus taught His disciples something very different in Matthew 18. He said if your brothers or sisters sin against you, go to them. If they listen to you, you have won them over. Peter sinned against Jesus and Jesus came to Peter to forgive him and win him over. Jesus also went to Peter to heal him, forgive him, and to restore him. If Peter was to grow and become the "rock" that Jesus said he was to be, Jesus had to recommission him and call him again. So Jesus asked Peter if he loved Him. His responses empowered Peter to return to ministry. The three questions could relate to Peter's three denials. What we do know is that Jesus blotted out Peter's denials and Peter needed this if he was to carry out the work Jesus called him to. Jesus was assuring him of his calling. Jesus renewed in him the authority to preach and teach.

This is good news for us as well! Restoration was necessary. If Jesus had not blotted out Peter's sin the message of grace would have been canceled. We desperately need to hear this message of grace. We need to see Peter coming forth as a new man. We need also to know that Jesus can make us new, that the grace of Jesus Christ is as much for us today as it was for Peter then. Jesus recalled Peter and said, "Follow Me." He did this so Peter would know to continue the work Jesus called him to do. Peter got stronger and stronger in Christ after he was recommissioned. More and more, day by day, he did become the "rock." He may have stumbled along the way just as we do, but the name the Master had given him became reality.

In the story of Peter, Jesus broke the denial. Today, it is the work of the Holy Spirit to break denial and when He does, He swoops in to comfort and heal just as Jesus did with Peter.

Now, it's time for a little application. We are going to work through some things we may have denied, but the good news is that truth will set us free!

1. Are you experiencing denial now?
2. What are you denying?
3. Trace the events of your painful experience. At the time, what was going on in your mind and thoughts?
4. Sometimes it can be difficult to accept our pain and the circumstances surrounding it. Do you feel like you have embraced this acceptance?
5. What were your fears at the time of your painful experience?
6. What can you no longer deny about your experience?

Let's talk a little bit about guilt. I like to call it the silent killer. Guilt robs us of so much: our peace, our joy, and our freedom. We suffer under self-condemnation. It's good to remember that our feelings and perception of ourselves are not how we are viewed by our heavenly Father.

> *"Always filter the external through the Eternal*
> *before allowing it to become internal."*
> —STEVE MCVEY

7. What does Paul tell us in Romans 8:1? Write this promise out in entirety below and meditate on it.

The Recommission

8. Now, let's return to our friend Peter and his beautiful story of restoration. What does Jesus tell Peter to do in John chapter 21 at the end of verse 17?

In 2020, I traveled to Israel and was blessed to stand on the very shoreline where Peter swam towards Jesus and approached Him after the denial. Standing in the very place where Peter was recommissioned was humbling to say the least. I felt my knees wanting to lower to the ground. Looking across the water you could envision that moment when Peter was fishing and recognizes Jesus standing on the shore and leaps into the water—"It is the Lord!"—then rushing towards His embrace.

Now, this is profound to me because Peter was one of Jesus' closest disciples. Remember, after Jesus was rejected and left Nazareth, He went to live in Capernaum with Peter and his mother-in-law. Peter may have spoken to Jesus more than any other disciple. Can you imagine the relationship? If so, then you can imagine the mournful heart Peter had after denying Jesus three times! After denying Jesus, Peter went back to doing the only thing he knew to do: fishing. After Peter reaches Jesus on the shore, Jesus asked Peter three times, "Do you love Me?" The third time Jesus asked Peter, the Bible says Peter was hurt. I can only imagine the sound of Peter's defeated voice when he said, "Lord, you know all things; you know that I love you" (John 21:17 NIV).

Then Jesus tells him to "feed My lambs, take care of My sheep.... Follow Me! Jesus recommissioned Peter, because He saw his heart, and He sees our hearts too! I find it very comforting that in all of our mistakes, God sees our heart.

He knows when we truly love Him, and He will seek us out just like He did Peter, and He will recommission us, again and again, to do His work!

9. What is Jesus telling you now?

Turn your trials into testimonies, and your struggles into stories that can help others. Go feed His sheep!

What does that look like for you? Well, it might be talking to a friend, a neighbor, a child, or a coworker. It may be a one-on-one conversation, a group discussion, or a message presented on a platform in front of thousands, but whatever God gives you, just say *yes!* and you will feed His sheep.

My brother, Bennie, who is now in heaven, knew what it was like to run away. He ran from many things. Escape and denial were very evident in his life, but in the end, he said, "It doesn't matter where you go, but who's beside you that counts." Make Jesus your driver in this journey on earth and you will reach an eternal destination.

I want to share a poem my brother wrote. He titled it "Success."

The road to success is not straight. There is a curve called failure, a loop called confusion, speed bumps called friends, red lights called enemies, caution lights called family. You will have flats called jobs, but if you have a spare called determination, an engine called perseverance, insurance called faith, and a driver called Jesus, you will make it to a place called success.

Now, in this moment, Jesus says, "I love you. I have come to recommission you. Stop running; stop trying to escape." I ask the Holy Spirit to break any form of denial right now. Jesus says,

"You are My beloved whom I have chosen to feed My sheep. I have called you by name. Thou art Mine."

Now go and do that which He has called you to do, in Jesus' name, amen!

Love Letter #3

My Dearest Child,

Now that you are fully grasping some things that I need to teach you, let Me examine your heart for any remaining denial or guilt. Sit quietly in My presence.

I have provided a safe place for you to face denial and release any guilt placed upon your heart so it never has the opportunity to condemn you again. This is a process, but as long as you are willing, My Spirit will do the work. Now, quiet your heart and thoughts and allow Me to show you anything that may be holding you in bondage. I know it is hard work, but I am with you and I uphold you in My righteous right hand. This process is meant to bring what has been hiding in the darkness for so long out into the light, so that I may begin to heal you! I look upon you with love.

Love,

Your Heavenly Father

CHAPTER 5

A Visitor Named Anger

Don't give into worry or anger;
it only leads to trouble.
—PSALM 37:8 GNT

E very day we are faced with tough situations that can call
forth different reactions from each of us. Some might be
sad; others may grow angry. Even though these emotions
are perfectly normal, especially through a grieving process, God
meant for them to be visitors, never residents in our hearts. In
the Bible, God advises us to let go of our anger as soon as possible, because intense anger can lead to sin.

1. Read Hebrews 12:15. What does it say about bitterness?
2. What does King Solomon teach us in Ecclesiastes 7:9?
3. What are we told to do in Proverbs 29:11?

So many relationships are damaged in the name of "offense."
We are so quickly offended, but Scripture tells us that a person's
wisdom yields to patience, and it is to one's glory and advantage
to overlook an offense. I love this version: "If you are sensible,

you will control your temper. When someone wrongs you, it is a great virtue to ignore it" (Prov. 19:11 GNT).

This is a good time to dive into our next love letter!

Love Letter #4

My Dearest Child,

Let Me examine your heart for any anger. You have every right to be angry. Anger is a very powerful emotion. Denial and anger are used to help us cope with a loss. Anger is one of the strongest of human passions. Anger does not go away on its own. If denied, it finds unhealthy ways to express itself and tends to form roots of bitterness that you may or may not be able to recognize. I created the emotion of anger, but there is a difference between the righteous anger felt by My Son, and unrighteous anger. I want to teach you the guidelines I have set for you to follow concerning anger. I will teach you loving and constructive ways to deal with your emotions. I will give you patience and wisdom to handle every situation.

I want you to begin to release any anger so it never has the opportunity to control you again. This is a choice you must make, but as long as you are willing, My Spirit will do the work. Now, be still, quiet your thoughts, and allow Me to cleanse your heart of any resentment and bitterness. I will show you where this pain originated and remove it from your soul. I will teach you how certain traps can entangle you, and how you can be free from them. I will fill you with My peace and grace and you will become a person of peace and grace!

Love,

Your Heavenly Father

4. Let's begin to identify and tackle any unresolved anger that may be camping out in our hearts. On a separate piece of paper, write down the names of any people you could be holding anger against in regard to your experience.

This could be anyone who harmed you, or whom you believe influenced your decisions or experiences. Write down their names and then order them according to the depth of anger. For example: 5 indicating the most anger, down to 1 for the least.

You may also need to list by multiple experiences, if you have had more than one trauma or pain in your life. At any rate, let the anger flood your paper. Leave nothing and no one out. You can use red paper or a red sharpie. A little creativity might make the exercise more enjoyable. As hard as it can be, I want you to also rejoice, because anger is leaving your camp. You are saying bye-bye to anger. It is check out time! This is something to celebrate.

At this point, it is good to be reminded that we are doing this work because there are some things in your heart that need to come out. These things have been taking up space where the goodness of God needs to flow. So, we want to remove the bad things and replace them with the good things. Let me explain. . . .

God cares deeply about the condition of our heart. The issue of the heart is a critical one. Physically speaking, without a healthy heart, we die. Spiritually speaking, the same is true.

One day I was cleaning out my refrigerator and God began to speak to me about the issues of the heart. He said, "Jeannie, just like you're cleaning this fridge, so the heart needs to be cleaned." You see, I love to clean out my fridge before I go grocery shopping. I want it super clean and here is why. Sometimes there are things that sit in there too long and they begin to spoil or mold. Some things are out of date and unhealthy for me to digest. Sometimes there are things way back in the back, almost hidden, that need to come out and I didn't even know they were in there. Things that are bad, taking up space, and needing to be thrown away. After everything is cleaned out, I will take a clean sanitizing cloth and wipe it all perfectly clean. This makes me feel so good. Why? Because now I am headed to the store to purchase loads of healthy foods for my family. I am going to fill the fridge and because I first cleaned it out, there is plenty of room. Now, it will be filled with good things that will bless my family.

Our hearts are the same. We need to clean them out. When we get rid of the bad stuff like anger, bitterness, and negativity, then the good stuff can take its place—like peace, joy, patience, and self-control. If we don't do the clean-out, the bad things stay in, pollute the good things, and make us sick from digesting them.

I was so thankful for the fridge analogy God gave me. It came just in time as I was soon to leave for a speaking engagement at a women's retreat. The topic was the heart. It was helpful for them, and I hope it will be helpful for you also.

5. What does Proverbs 14:14 tell us?
6. What does Paul tell us to do with evil in Romans 12:21?
7. What instructions does James give in chapter 1:19–20 in dealing with a situation that could be a trap for anger?
8. Read James 4:1–2. These verses encourage us to examine our hearts for any war possibly raging inside us. As we do this, it's also important to identify what type of anger we have. Do you explode or implode?

Here are some examples of **exploding anger:** shouting, property damage, physical fights, throwing objects, intense arguments, temper tantrums, profanity, threats, assaults, road rage, and even murder.

Here are some examples of **imploding anger:** sadness,

depression, isolation, pouting, withdrawal, sarcasm, defensiveness, cynicism, conflict avoidance, control, muscle tension, headaches, complaining, negative mindset, difficulty in boundaries.

What type of anger did you witness in your home as a child?

This is a great question, because acting in anger can be a learned behavior. When I discovered this, I felt a load fall off. At least now there was a good possible reason for my responses to things going on around me. This becomes generational. There is a good chance that the way conflict was handled in your childhood home was the way it was handled in your parents' homes as well.

Daily ask God to search your heart so no anger can take root.

I recently heard a woman speak on the topic of anger. She stated she was one of nine children and anger was ever-present in her home and it came from her dad. She said she spent a lifetime just trying to figure out what he was so mad about, but she never could. She went on to share that all her siblings were deeply affected by the anger. Then she made this statement and it rattled me. She said, "My dad left a legacy of anger." Can you imagine one of your children saying that about you? Oh Lord, let it never be.

If you are someone who battles anger on a daily basis, stop right now and pray.

Lord, please deliver me from this anger. Cleanse my heart. Show me where this pain originates and remove it from my soul. Show me how to deal with my anger in a healthy way and keep me from causing any pain. Lord, uproot it and fill me instead with Your peace. Teach me to be a person of peace and grace. Show me how to overcome and be free. In Jesus' name, amen.

My Declaration: I choose this day that anger will not be my legacy.

Signature: _____

Date:_____

9. Now let's look at a healthy, biblical example of anger. Jesus was righteous and expressed righteous anger. What made Him angry in the following passages?

    Mark 3:1–6

    John 2:13–16

10. What anger have you been able to identify?

11. Read Ephesians 4:30–31. What do you need to do with any anger now?

Jesus did not sin when He was angry. He had self-control. He tells us to follow that example. "In your anger do not sin. Do not let the sun go down while you are still angry" (Eph. 4:26 NIV).

Daily ask God to search your heart so no anger can take root. This simple practice will be worth its weight in gold. Speaking of gold, I will share this quote with you written by my daddy:

> *It would be nice to have pockets of gold,*
> *but the heart in the end is worth much more.*
> — THOMAS EUGENE SCOTT

I think he nailed it. There is nothing more important than our heart. King Solomon, known as the wisest man, said it best: "Above all else, guard your heart, for everything you do flows from it" (Prov. 4:23 NIV).

I think you're ready for your next exercise. Go back to the list you created of all the people you hold anger towards. One by one, I want you to call their names and say the following out loud.

"I release any anger I have towards _____. I will no longer allow this anger to control me."

Feel free to customize if needed. It's important that you make this personal, but vital to verbally call out the names and release the anger. By verbalizing you are declaring that these names and circumstances no longer have power over you. Now, I should mention as you do this exercise you may not *feel* that the anger is gone, but that's okay; it's a process and you just opened the door to freedom through your words. There is power in your words. As a believer, your words have the power to set you free. Remember, your very salvation depended on you "confessing" your sins and then believing upon Jesus as your Lord and Savior. Isn't that awesome? Your words brought you into a relationship with the Messiah that gives you eternal life!

We cannot rely on emotions and what we "feel." We must rely on truth! So truth must always lead us, and feelings come later.

Once you've completed the exercise, celebrate! Keep a copy. We will need it in the next chapter, but you may want to rip up the original paper your names were written on, burn it, dig a hole in your back yard, or whatever you want to do! I get it! It's your story and there are some details you just get to add for yourself.

At the end of the day, we want a healthy, whole heart, set free from anger. We want the bountiful goodness, and the healing of God to flow. This is my prayer for you. Anger will not be your legacy. I realize this could be just the beginning of your breakthrough. If anger is something you struggle with, seek additional counseling, because anger is a serious issue and needs serious attention.

Anger is an acid that can do more harm to
the vessel in which it is stored than to
anything on which it is poured.
— MARK TWAIN

CHAPTER 6

I Just Can't Forgive Myself

In him we have redemption through his
blood, the forgiveness of sins, in accordance
with the riches of God's grace.

—EPHESIANS 1:7 NIV

So many times I have heard the expression, "I just can't forgive myself." Guess what? I have good news for you! You don't have to. As a matter of fact, it is impossible to forgive yourself. Forgiveness is a gift that Jesus died to give you. All you have to do is accept it. Many individuals think they are having difficulty forgiving themselves when actually they are just having difficulty accepting the gift of forgiveness. When Christ said on the cross, "It is finished," He meant it is finished! He was the prefect sacrifice, the spotless lamb given for you and me. If someone gives you a gift, do you give it back and say, "No, thank you"? No, you simply accept it and say, "Thank you." That is what Jesus wants us to do with the gift of forgiveness. If we try to take on the job of forgiving ourselves then we are actually denying the finished work on the cross.

What separates us from freedom and from applying this truth to our lives is wrong teaching or wrong thinking about our identity. In reality, we have the head knowledge that God forgives all sins, but this message can't seem to reach our heart, which in turn makes it difficult to apply to our lives. Many times, the roadblock to freedom is in our mind. In this chapter, we are going to align our thoughts with God's. We are going to soak in the truth that nothing can separate us from the love of God (Rom. 8:38).

It's important to note that there is a big difference between forgiveness and healing. While forgiveness can be instantaneous for some people, healing is a process that takes time. Healing comes as forgiveness is extended. When we think about forgiveness, we should see the cross. Through the cross we see the vertical and horizontal forgiveness that Jesus established. Because of what Christ has done for us there is a vertical forgiveness. This takes place as many times as we need it between us on earth and Jesus, who sits as our mediator in heaven at the right hand of the Father. That forgiveness gives us the power to then forgive horizontally all those around us. In both directions, we can experience freedom!

Once I was speaking at a ladies' luncheon and I shared this truth. Afterwards, as some of the ladies were greeting me, I noticed an elderly lady in the back. She was circling tables, and I distinctly noticed how she hung her head. After the room cleared, she walked up to me and said, "Honey, I was invited to come here today, and I didn't want to come, but I am so glad I did. I have been waiting all my life to hear what you said today." She was seventy-two years old and had been trapped in torment through the years trying to forgive herself and needing to understand the gift of God through His Son, Jesus. She needed to understand there was nothing wrong with her; she just needed to heal.

On another occasion, I shared this truth with a fifty-four-year-old woman. Instantly, before my very eyes, I saw a physical transformation take place as the light bulbs went on and chains fell away. She said, "All this time I thought something was wrong with me because I couldn't seem to forgive myself." To which I replied, "My sweet sister, Jesus never required this of you. It was out of His great love He gifted it to you." Let's hear more from the Father in the following love letter to you.

My Dearest Child,

Your journey to freedom is through choosing to forgive. Forgiveness belongs to Me. The idea of forgiveness originated with Me. I sent My Son, Jesus, to be the sacrifice for ALL sins. It is through Him that all people are offered forgiveness. My child, this forgiveness is a gift to you, and because you have been forgiven you can now choose to share this forgiveness with others.

I no longer want you to be bound by the sins of others. Nor do I want you to be bound up with bitterness in your heart toward others. They know not what they do. They know not what they have done. Leave their circumstances to Me.

Are you ready to fully forgive those who have hurt you? The time is now! Turn away. I will flood your heart with My peace. I will make a way for you to move forward, out of your place of confinement and into the fullness of life lived in Christ. Forgiveness is what I require from you, but remember, I will not command you to do something that I will not enable you to do.

Accept this gracious gift, and then gift it to others! Bear with each other and forgive whatever grievances you may have against one another. Forgive as I have forgiven you (Col. 3:13).

Love,

Your Heavenly Father

*When we choose to forgive, God sends
the grace to do the healing.*
—VINITA HAMPTON WRIGHT

Forgiveness cannot be proven by our feelings. Forgiveness is a choice, not an emotion. We first choose to forgive, then the feelings follow. Not the other way around. We cannot rely on feelings; we must rely on truth!

1. How far does God go to remove our sins? Read Psalm 103:12.
2. Does God remember our sins? Read Hebrews 8:12.
3. God does not remember our sins, but He doesn't allow us to forget. I have often wondered why. I have come to believe that the memory of our past sins and hurts provides a powerful platform to minister to other hurting people. So, it is that our past mistakes and the radical grace and healing God has provided us now become an extended gift to others.

   Forgiveness cannot be proven by our feelings. Forgiveness is a choice, not an emotion.

4. Think of those involved with your painful experience. Whom do you need to forgive? Sit quietly with God. Ask Him to bring every person to mind. Refer back to your anger list. The same names typically may apply here and God may reveal new ones. Use this space to list the names.

Harboring unforgiveness in our heart towards someone actually harms us, not them. You may have heard the saying, "Unforgiveness is like drinking poison and hoping someone else would die." It is so true. It harms us, not the other.

5. Do you set limitations or standards for forgiving others?

What are they?

For example: "I will forgive _____ when_____ or if
_____."

If you do, you may be waiting a long time. Our standards usually don't come to fruition. However, Jesus defines His standards.

6. What standards does Luke 17:3–4 give?
7. What does Luke 6:35–36 instruct us to do?
8. Paul is very clear on how we must forgive. What does he say in Colossians 3:13?
9. Our very own fellowship with God and our forgiveness depends on us forgiving others. What does Mark 11:25 say?
10. Can you imagine God denying you the forgiveness of your sins? How does the thought impact you?

The way I see it, the greatest opportunity to share the gospel is through forgiveness. I remember the day I was faced with a decision to forgive or not. I heard the Lord whisper, "Forgive now, just as I forgave you." In that moment, the mercy He poured over me from the sin of my abortion flashed before my eyes.

When we forgive we mirror Christ. Through forgiveness, we experience the fullness of God's grace. Take a moment and ask God to show you any unforgiveness remaining in your heart.

11. Read Matthew 18:21–35. What do verses 33 and 35 say?
12. What does Ephesians 4:32 then tell you to do?

Take some time to meditate on the cross where He was wounded for your sins. Now, take some time to thank Him that by His stripes you are healed. Thank Him for the gift of forgiveness. Thank Him for His glorious love. Be reconciled to God though His Son, Jesus Christ, rejoicing in the truth that nothing can separate you from His love! How beautiful it is! He adores you!

In case you're still struggling with forgiving yourself, let's align our thoughts once more. Thinking we must forgive ourselves indicates that we either doubt God's forgiveness through His Son, or we just don't believe we are worthy enough to receive it. Pride could also be a hindrance. Have we ascended to the throne and made ourself judge? In this case, we need to ask for forgiveness for attempting to take Jesus' seat of authority. All ideas are lies of the enemy. Forgiveness is not something you can do for yourself. If we could do it ourselves, why would we need a Savior? It is a gift that has been purchased for you. Forgiveness died and rose again for you and me. Choose today to honor our Lord by fully receiving His gift of forgiveness. "So if the Son sets you free, you will be free indeed" (John 8:36 NIV).

13. Will you now receive the gift of forgiveness? You have to choose. Reach out and take it!

Now, let's end this chapter strong! We are free from indwelling sin!

14. What do the following verses declare?
    Romans 8:1
    Romans 8:28
    Romans 8:32
    Romans 8:33
    Romans 8:34
    Romans 8:37

Romans 8:38–39

Now, let's take some action towards our freedom. Look at the list of names you made in the previous chapter. These will typically be individuals you also need to forgive, but there could be others. Matter of fact, God may be revealing other names to you right now in this moment. So, pause and listen, but remember you cannot add your name to the list, because as you have learned, you cannot forgive yourself. Once you have your completed list, say the following out loud:

"I forgive _____ for _____
_____. I will no longer allow this person, these memories, or these feelings to control or manipulate me anymore."

For some of you this is extremely difficult. What you have gone through was deeply painful and you feel like you will never be able to forgive and maybe have even said so. But remember, forgiveness is not for the other person; it is for you. Forgiveness does not mean you allow ongoing pain or suffering. For example: Someone may have abused you in some way. Just because you forgive them does not mean they can continue to harm you, or that you have to stay in a position to allow them to.

The other thing to know is that with forgiveness there is not always reconciliation. Many times reconciliation does not or cannot happen, but that's not needed for your freedom. Let me give you another example. Once I was counseling a mother who lost her daughter to suicide. The mother was struggling with guilt. She desperately wished she could talk with her daughter and reconcile, but her daughter was gone. Nevertheless, this mother needed to be set free. Her very life depended on it. So, one day during one of our sessions, I had her speak out to her daughter as if she was in the room. I asked her, what would you like to say to your daughter? I pulled up a chair as if her daughter was sitting there. The mother began to sweat and shake as she spoke. She was being delivered. Though reconciliation was not possible, she was able to tell her daughter she was sorry and ask for her forgiveness. Giving her the opportunity to verbalize these things set her free from the bondage she was in.

Extending forgiveness and accepting forgiveness sets YOU free! If you are still struggling with forgiving, let me give you a visual.

Imagine yourself walking around all the time with a heavy bag filled with stones wrapped around your neck. For the sake of analogy, we will call this weight the "bag of unforgiveness." It has become a huge burden, because it is with you everywhere you go. The heaviness has your head lowered and your spine out of alignment. You are in desperate need of rehab. The pain and discomfort is growing by the day. It is affecting your health and functional abilities. This "bag of unforgiveness" is draining you, paralyzing you, and eventually could kill you, because of the strain it's putting on all the other vital parts of your body, soul, and spirit. What is one to do? Seek a physician, the greatest physician, Jesus. Allow Him to heal you. Of course, you play a role in the healing process too. You have to be willing to remove what is making you weary and sick. You have to be willing to see the Physician.

I will share one more story with you. One of the greatest forgiveness stories we can learn from is the one of Corrie Ten Boom. Here is what she writes:

It was in a church in Munich that I saw him—a balding, heavyset man in a gray overcoat, a brown felt hat clutched between his hands. People were filing out of the basement room where I had just spoken, moving along the rows of wooden chairs to the door at the rear. It was 1947 and I had come from Holland to defeated Germany with the message that God forgives.

It was the truth they needed most to hear in that bitter, bombed-out land, and I gave them my favorite mental picture. Maybe because the sea is never far from a Hollander's mind, I liked to think that's where forgiven sins were thrown. "When we confess our sins," I said, "God casts them into the deepest ocean, gone forever."

The solemn faces stared back at me, not quite daring to believe. People stood up in silence, in silence collected their wraps, in silence left the room.

And that's when I saw him, working his way forward against the others. One moment I saw the overcoat and the brown hat; the next, a blue uniform and a visored cap with its skull and crossbones. It came back with a rush: the huge room with its harsh overhead lights; the pathetic pile of dresses and shoes in the center of the floor; the shame of walking naked past this man. I could see my sister's frail form ahead of me, ribs sharp beneath the parchment skin. *Betsie, how thin you were!*

My sister Betsie and I had been arrested for concealing Jews in our home during the Nazi occupation of Holland; this man had been a guard at Ravensbruck concentration camp where we were sent.

Now he was in front of me, hand thrust out: "A fine message, how good it is to know that, as you say, all our sins are at the bottom of the sea!"

And I, who had spoken so glibly of forgiveness, fumbled in my pocketbook rather than take his hand. He would not remember me, of course—how could he remember one prisoner among those thousands of women?

But I remembered him and the leather crop swinging from his belt. I was face-to-face with one of my captors and my blood seemed to freeze.

"You mentioned Ravensbruck in your talk," he said, "I was a guard there." No, surely, he did not remember me.

"But since that time," he went on, "I have become a Christian. I know that God has forgiven me for the cruel things I did there, but I would like to hear it from your lips as well. *Fräulein*,"—again, the hand came out—"will you forgive me?"

And I stood there—I whose sins had again and again been forgiven—and I could not forgive. Betsie had died in that place—could he erase her slow terrible death simply by the asking?

It could not have been many seconds that he stood there—hand held out—but to me it seemed hours as I wrestled with the most difficult thing I had ever had to do.

For I had to do it—I knew that. The message that God forgives has a prior condition: that we forgive those who have injured us. If you do not forgive men their trespasses, Jesus says, neither will your Father in heaven forgive your trespasses.

I stood there with coldness clutching my heart, but forgiveness is not an emotion—I knew that too. Forgiveness is an act of the will, and the will can function regardless of the temperature of the heart. "Help!" I prayed silently. "I can lift my hand. I can do that much, but I need you to supply the feeling."

And so woodenly, mechanically, I thrust my hand into

the one stretched out to me. And as I did, an incredible thing took place. The current started in my shoulder, raced down my arm, sprang into our joined hands. And then this healing warmth seemed to flood my whole being, bringing tears to my eyes. "I forgive you, brother!" I cried. "With all my heart!'"

For a long moment we grasped each other's hands, the former guard and the former prisoner. I had never known God's love so intensely, as I did then.

(Taken from "I'm Still Learning to Forgive" by Corrie ten Boom.)

Forgiveness is the key that unlocks the doors to power! Forgiveness opens the flood gates for wounds to heal and breaks the bondage of offenses. It brings life to the soul and health to the bones. It's a mighty tool of God to bring healing all around in every circumstance. It stops the enemy cold, because it is a reflection of Christ—His identity, and our identity. Forgive others, not because they deserve it, but because you deserve it. You deserve peace.

The Glory of Christianity is to
conquer by forgiveness.
—WILLIAM BLAKE

When we forgive, we give a sinner
like ourselves another chance and
we free ourselves to live and grow in
the bountiful grace of God.
—VINITA HAMPTON WRIGHT

CHAPTER 7

Goodbye Depression

The LORD is a refuge for the oppressed, a
stronghold in times of trouble.
—PSALM 9:9 (NIV)

When our pain and grief are not dealt with, we can turn our emotions inward. We try to cope with our pain in silence and alone, but the grief and pain become unbearable and depression sets in. Individuals may punish themselves through self-destruction, self-pity, and self-condemnation. Notice the word "self." Everything turns inward, because you can't identify a safe place to pour out the pain. There is shame and a fear of judgment, so you develop "inward eyeballs." The result is a wrecked identity. Many times, the depression leads to suicidal thoughts, but there is good news!

He sent His word and healed them, And
delivered them from their destructions.
—PSALM 107:20 (NKJV)

This is by far my favorite Scripture for depression. We have already talked about unforgiveness and guilt, but I find it important to mention it once more here. Unforgiveness keeps us from being able to live in the goodness of God, and guilt keeps us in continual pain. If the two are not dealt with, they collide and lead to depression. They lead ultimately to a prison of bondage where the enemy plans to keep you locked. Praise God we are going to discover the key to freedom!

Love Letter #6

Dearest Child,

Together, we have come a long way. I am so proud of you and, oh, how I deeply love and care for you. We are nearing the end of this journey only to begin a new journey! We are going to take a look at depression. The enemy puts so many of My children in the bondage of depression. As we review what it is, I only want you to focus on the tool I give you, My Word, which SETS YOU FREE! As you review My Scriptures, decide which verses you will remember when times of depression or anxiety come. Then, enter the battle and take victory over these foes! Remember, the enemy is a thief, but My Son, Jesus, came so that you may have life and have it abundantly (John 10:10).

Lastly, do not allow yourself to be so buried in your past that you can't see your promised future. I want you to rest in My Word. I want you to believe and obey. If you do this, you will be delivered from all emotional bondage and begin to walk in the light of My love and plan for your life.

Love,

Your Heavenly Father

Let's examine our hearts and identify the root cause of depression. If your depression had a voice, what would is say about you? Depression is an active, real experience and can result from many sources, including guilt due to unconfessed sin, shame, anxiety, fears, bitterness, unforgiveness, unfulfilled expectations, and hopeless grieving. Many of these sources surround pain, especially hopeless grieving, but praise God we are learning there is actually great hope found in our grieving. These sources now become lies. Lies used to harm us, but lies we can overcome with truth!

1. Read Psalm 32:1–5. What did King David say delivered him?

Forgiveness brings true joy. Only when we ask God to forgive our sins will He give us real joy and relief from guilt.

2. Have you confessed all your sins?

Go ahead and take a moment and let the Holy Spirit search your heart. Confess anything He may reveal to you. Now, grab hold of your forgiveness, your freedom, and accept it fully. He finished the complete work on the cross and paid fully for all our sins. We just have to accept it! It's a gift!

3. How might God use your personal suffering to help or heal others?

As you ponder this answer, let's talk a bit about suffering. There are many things that cause suffering and many ways it could be defined. Elizabeth Elliot describes suffering as "having what you don't want or wanting what you don't have." I can tell you that some of things I have learned at the deepest level came through my suffering. I can also tell you some of the greatest gifts have come through suffering. For example: love, motherhood, ministry, grief, and loss. Of course, when you're going through suffering it certainly does not feel like a gift. It's later that God allows you to see how He used the suffering to help others, to grow you, to bless you, and to bless others. At the appropriate time, He does bring beauty from the ashes.

God does not want us to suffer, but suffering is a part of life. One must not forget—Jesus endured the greatest suffering known to man. We see through His suffering the greatest gift given to mankind: salvation and eternal life. Through His suffering we could all be forgiven. The most painful sacrifice in human history became the greatest gift to the world. Because He was human, He knows exactly what our suffering is like and He is eager to heal us all. Remember, by His stripes we are healed! So, to understand suffering, we have to first understand the love of God.

To reflect on a biblical example, we can certainly explore Job. Job was a good and righteous man and one would expect nothing but blessings and favor to envelop him. Then Job lost everything. The life he lived turned upside down and seemed more like living under a curse than a blessing. He lost all his children, his livestock, his servants, his home, his health. Job did not have an answer for the suffering he was going through, yet he trusted God and he was patient in his suffering. He never doubted God existed, even through his harsh remarks and honest complaints to God. We can learn much from Job. Could it be that God allowed this story to be recorded so that it may be our very survival kit today?

And, of course, you know how the story ends. Job was given back everything he lost and more. So, once again, through the suffering, the gift arises. Through the suffering, even you and I are blessed today through the story of Job. It gives us hope as we await our gift through our own suffering.

Once I was going through some very painful times in ministry. I experienced the sting of rejection, betrayal, and loss. The pain paralyzed me at times. I began to ask God to help me understand suffering. I ran across a quote by Elizabeth Elliot that read, "Suffering is a mystery. It is not explained, but it is affirmed. And we must remember that all Christianity rests on mysteries."

Elizabeth Elliot was no stranger to suffering. Most of her life she experienced it and we can learn a lot from her ministry. Her first husband was speared to death after he arrived in a village where he hoped to share the gospel. Her second husband was lost to cancer and there were other sorrows. All of this led her to say, "Whatever is in the cup that God is offering to me, whether it be pain and sorrow and suffering and grief along with the many more joys, I'm willing to take it because I trust Him. Because suffering is never for nothing."

> *"Suffering is a mystery. It is not explained, but it is affirmed. And we must remember that all Christianity rests on mysteries."*
>
> ELIZABETH ELLIOT

Kind of sounds like Job, doesn't it? Now what might our response be?

I wanted to take what I was learning and apply it to my life. I developed a habit in my life that has been super helpful. No matter what I am going through, I ask myself a couple of questions: First, what can I learn from this? And second, where is Jesus in this moment? Where is Jesus in the suffering? Keep your eyes on Him. He will carry you through, because, I promise, He has His eyes carefully on you. He comes to us in our times of trouble and sorrow and if we press in and listen, we can hear Him say, "Trust Me. Walk with Me."

4. Read 1 John 4:4. What indication does it give to the source of your victory?
5. Let's consider Joseph. What does Genesis 50:20 say?

Joseph was thrown into a pit, and later into prison. He knew all too well what it was like being in a pit. Later, we see how God honored him and used him for greatness. The story of Joseph reminds us that Satan would like nothing better than to throw us all in a pit, especially someone with a godly vision into a pit of despair, so be on guard!

6. Can you identify unexpressed thoughts or feelings surrounding your painful experience that could have led to your depression?
7. Are there any thoughts that still haunt you in regard to your pain?
8. Have you had suicidal thoughts? If so, what were you hoping suicide would accomplish for you?
9. Read Numbers 11:10–17. Moses wants to die, because his burden is so heavy, but instead what is God's response?
10. Read 1 Kings 19:4–18. Elijah wants to die, but instead what does God do?
11. Read Proverbs 12:25. What does it directly tell us causes depression?
12. Where can we turn when we have a heart full of anxiety? (Psa. 50:15).
13. Read Matthew 11:28–30. Which part gives you the greatest comfort?

14. How do the following Scriptures prove God's love and
    care for you?
    Psalm 34:18
    Psalm 56:8
- Have you grieved your loss (if this applies)?
- Do you still feel shame in regard to your painful
  experience?
- What promises can you claim in the following verses?
  2 Corinthians 7:9–11
  Isaiah 61:7

I love that! Double for your trouble! I have listed some more
passages here that you may find helpful. I like to call them:

God's Remedy for Depression
- Allow others to help carry your burden (Gal. 6:2).
- Focus on God and others instead of yourself (Isa. 26:3).
- Confess any sin (Psa. 32:5).
- Set your mind on the things above (Col. 3:2).
- Renew your mind daily by prayer and reading God's
  Word (Rom. 12:2).
- Let our attitude be the same of Christ (Phil. 2:5).
- Speak your identity (Eph. chapters 1, 2).
- Cast your cares upon the Lord (1 Pet. 5:7).
- Pray with thanksgiving (1 Thess. 5:16-18).
- Speak peace over your life (Rom. 15:13).
- Praise and worship the Lord (Psa. 7:17).

Determine now which passage you will cling to when the
enemy tries to put you in the pit. Remember, Jesus fought and
overcame the enemy with the Word of God and we can too! So, it
is with a sound mind that we say, "Goodbye, Depression!"

I waited patiently for the Lord; He turned to
me and heard my cry. He lifted me out of the
slimy pit, out of the mud and mire; He set
my feet on a rock and gave me a firm place
to stand. He put a new song in my mouth, a
hymn of praise to our God. Many will see and
fear and put their trust in the Lord.

—PSALM 40:1-3 NIV

As we conclude this chapter, I want to say to you that I understand the stronghold of depression. It is a serious issue and should be addressed properly. I have battled it much in my own life. This black hole, this demonic thing we call depression, has also impacted many of my family members and ultimately was the core root causing me to lose both my daddy and brother. So, I am no friend to depression. Depression is the enemy. It is the opposite of the abundant life Jesus wants all His children to live. Depression is a tool of Satan, the father of lies, to keep you in a hopeless, bottomless pit, but let me tell you there is no pit too dark or deep that Jesus, our mighty Defender, can't snatch you out of! You are not out of His reach ever. So, look up, see the light, feel His love. He sings and dances over you. You are His beloved. Look up; take His hand. Nothing is impossible for Him and those who believe (Matt. 19:26).

I also understand there are times when additional help is needed such as medication and ongoing counseling. I have walked that path also, and know that you can be free. I wholeheartedly believe God gives us the needed tools, wisdom, and care both through His Word and the care and counsel of others who have overcome.

As I was writing this chapter, my seven-year-old son, Luke,

was upstairs and he began to sing and play on his guitar a little song he wrote. From the mouth of a babe, he titled it:

"We All Need Freedom"
We need healing, we need hope,
We need that freedom that sets us free.

We need that hope, we need that love,
We need that healing from above.

You may be sad, but God is listening,
You may be grieving, but God is listening,
It may be hard, but God is listening.

If you need hope then just pray,
You will be given what you need,
We all need freedom indeed.

Many times, after my daddy passed away, I would go into my prayer closet and cling to the lyrics in a song or Scriptures that gave me hope. I didn't realize until after he passed away just how deep his depression was and that knowledge intensified my grieving.

One night I was alone and crying so hard I could barely get my breath. There came a knock at the door, and when I opened it there was a package. Inside was a framed poem titled, "Don't Cry for Me," written by Deborah Garcia Gaitan.

As I read the words, I could hear my daddy's voice. It was as if he was reading it directly to me. It was during one of my deepest moments of sorrow that God had sent an angel to my door to drop this package. As it turns out, it was my neighbor, Teresa. She later told me she just felt compelled to bring me a sympathy gift at that particular moment. I know God sent her.

That night she played the role of an angel. As I sat staring at the poem, God whispered to me, "Jeannie, in his darkest hours, he was not alone. I was with him." God always knows just what we need and how to provide it. In Hebrews 13:5, He promises He will never leave us or forsake us.

Little did I know that only two years later, I would also unexpectedly lose my brother who also suffered from depression. I was not prepared for this devastating loss, but are we ever? The pain was so deep, so raw, and I longed for him. I wanted to know why this had to happen.

The Lord began to teach me more about one of the demonic forces employed by depression and it's called shame. Shame is different than guilt. Guilt is a message of "I did something bad." Shame is deeper. The message of shame is "I am bad." When we believe this lie, it takes deep root and begins to destroy our soul.

Shame causes you to isolate when you need relationships. It causes you to believe in a false identity of yourself. Shame occurs from many circumstances, but is often found in victims of abuse. When shameful and sinful acts have been committed, they attach themselves to the victim internally. This may be sins we committed ourselves or sins committed against us, but at any rate, it is a calculated work of Satan, our enemy. He wants to destroy our royal identity as children of God, but one day soon, Satan will pay the ultimate agonizing price for all the suffering he has caused. Glory!

Shame acts like a barrier and it keeps love from God and others from getting through. Shame causes you to believe the lie that you are unworthy of such love and relationship. Shame causes its victims to see the happiness and abundant life those around them may be experiencing, but they don't believe they are worthy of it themselves. Shame brings creativity, gifts, and talents to a halt, causes inability to express oneself, and makes you believe that you are imperfect and have to get yourself together before being presentable to others. Shame keeps you in a lonely, dark prison.

Shame is connected to depression, but there is freedom. There is healing. Jesus already covered shame on the cross. "Fear not, for you will not be put to shame ... you will not be disgraced ..." (Isa. 54:4 AMP). God speaks life and hope into shame. We see shame from the beginning with Adam and Eve. Satan tries to convince us we are not worthy of God's love and redemption. He convinces us God will not cover us. However, we see in Genesis 3:21 (NIV) that "the Lord God made garments from skin for Adam and his wife, and clothed them." With great love, He covered them. We must allow God to cover us.

Rather than covering ourselves with a false identity, one hidden in shame, we must run to God as we are naked and afraid. We must cry out to God, and it is here where He comforts us, covers us, and reminds us of the sacrifice of freedom that He has already made for us through His Son, Jesus. No matter where we have been, what we have done, or what has been done against us, His love is far-reaching, never failing, and ready to restore our true identity.

I was reminded of how God is always at work all around us in our lives and others'. We may not see it, but He is constantly weaving together a beautiful story of redemption. He uses our broken pieces, lives, and stories, and mends us all together. He uses our hurts and pains to comfort others if we are willing to be used for His glory.

I will leave you with yet another set of beautiful words written by Ailsa Yates titled, "Mosaic."

The Artist takes the broken bits,
He holds them in His hand,

And thinks of all the beauty,
He had for that life planned.

The Artist takes those broken bits,
And places them with care,
Among some other broken bits,
With whom He'd have them share.

And as these bits and pieces,
With His love are slowly joined,
We start to see the work of art,
That His great mind has coined.

Just like a great mosaic,
That only God can see,
He uses all His broken bits,
His people—you, and me.

For each of us are broken,
In one way or another,
But His love heals and binds us,

As His children, to each other.

We may not see the beauty,
In ourselves, or as a whole,
But we know that God is working,
To restore us, in His goal.

To be the perfect picture,
That always He has planned,
The lives of all His children,

Are held within His hand.

One day when we're in glory,
With Jesus by our side,
We'll see the finished picture,
look at it, from on High.

And we will see the beauty,
That God has always seen,
Instead of cracks dividing us,
It's God's love in between.

His love flows through His broken bits,
like a soft and healing glue,
He joins us and cements us,
In everything we do.

So don't discard the broken bits,
In your life, or in mine,
just know that there is a bigger plan,
That's made by God, divine.

Little did I know when I originally wrote this chapter and chose this poem, how much it would mean to me today. I'm beginning to realize more and more the reality of how heaven and earth work together, how the spiritual and physical realm come together for the master plan of God. I am comforted to know that I am working in union with the great cloud of witnesses (Heb. 12:1).

Sweet sister, God can take what is broken and make it whole again. He can turn ashes into beauty. He can make our hearts beat again. He can turn our grieving into joy. He can establish our steps and lift our heads. So, join me in rising up. Rise up my sister, rise up!

I pray over you and declare in the name of Jesus Christ that all strongholds of depression will be destroyed in your life. Speak this over yourself.

Confess and renounce any sin that could be holding you captive. Ask for God's forgiveness and receive it. The price has already been paid for you!

Release all individuals that have ever caused you pain or harm. Forgive them.

Speak to depression with authority and say, "Come out in the name of Jesus Christ!"

Lastly, ask the Father to fill that space with all His goodness.

May the goodness of God and His presence fill you and overtake you. May you be fully restored. May your inner being be strengthened. May you now experience freedom, peace, and joy, in Jesus' name, amen.

Now, sit still with the Lord. He is captivated by you. You are captivated by Him. Worship Him. Thank Him. Praise Him for all He has done, and for all He is going to do.

When gratitude becomes an essential
foundation in our lives, miracles start
to appear everywhere.
—EMMANUEL DAGHER

CHAPTER 8

I Am Free

I will sprinkle clean water on you, and you
will be clean; I will cleanse you from all your
impurities and from all your idols. I will give
you a new heart and put a new spirit within
you; I will remove from you your heart of
stone and give you a heart of flesh.

—EZEKIEL 36:25–26 NIV

Does the promise of a new heart and new spirit fill you with joy and anticipation? Oh, I hope so! God is in the process of breaking off any and all chains associated with your pain. The enemy put you in a place God never intended for you to be and now you are being SET FREE by the power of the Holy Spirit. I remember the moment Jesus reached down and touched me. It was a miracle in my life. I felt Him healing me. I felt Him tearing down my sick heart and rebuilding a healthy heart. He put a new heart and spirit in me and I have never been the same. He restored my self-image and crowned me as a princess. A sense of belonging to a royal family overwhelmed me. He has the same gift for you. He will present it differently, because it will have to be in a way you can receive it, but rest assured, He knows exactly what you need.

The price He paid for you to be free has been paid in full! Dear friend and sister, accept by faith His completed accomplishment on your behalf. "So, if the Son sets you free, you will be free indeed" (John 8:36 NIV).

There you have it. God said it in His Word, so it's final! Now we choose to believe in faith, by His grace. The feelings will follow, and this truth will be established in your mind and heart.

Love Letter #7

Dearest Child,

We will soon be approaching the end of this journey, but there will be many others. I want you to know that I have chosen you. I want you to know that I love you and I would leave the ninety-nine and rescue you over and over again to prove My love to you. I know everything about you and love you all the same. I call you daughter and I call you friend. I sent My Son so that you could be set free!

You are a gift to Me and to the world. You have not chosen Me, but I have chosen you so that you may go forth and bear much fruit (John 15:16). Nothing will ever change how I feel about you. I have good plans for you. After My healing work is complete in you, you will be completely set free to flow in My presence like a sweet perfume drawing others that need to hear the same good news!

Love,

Your Heavenly Father

The Woman at the Well

1. Read John 4:4. What does it say?

The story of the woman at the well is one of my favorites, partially because I am a woman, but much more because of the worth I needed spoken into my life, especially after my abortion. Jesus fulfilled that need for me just as He did for the Samaritan woman. What I want to specifically highlight first is that Scripture says Jesus "needed to go through Samaria." This touches me deeply every time I read it. **Jesus chose to go to her; He had to go to her.**

2. When Jesus reached Jacob's well, he sat down and rested. We are told in John 4:6 that He was weary from the journey. What time was it?

Now, we discover it was the hottest time of the day. The Samaritan woman came during this time of day because the other women did not want to be seen with her. She came during this time of day because she was despised, full of shame, condemned, and thought of herself as unworthy. Yet, **Jesus sat and waited for her.**

3. Where were the disciples? (John 4:8).

Jesus sent the disciples away. **Jesus wanted to be alone with her.**

4. What did she question Him on in John 4:9?

This encounter violated the cultural norms. **Jesus broke the rules to visit with her.**

Jesus was creating a great shift in mind, heart, and behavior. First, a Jewish man would not be found talking to a Samaritan woman. Second, He told her the day had come when worship would not be in the temple or on a mountain, but in Spirit and Truth. So, He was also breaking the barriers of custom and religion. He was painting a picture that God dies for everyone. He unites, not divides (John 4:19–24).

5. What did Jesus tell her in John 4:10?

He offered her living water. **Jesus brought her a gift!** He told her she would never thirst again, but have a fountain of water springing up into everlasting life (John 4:14).

6. What did Jesus begin to reveal to her concerning His knowledge of her past and current relationships? (John 4:16-18).

He knew all about her past, and every detail about her present and **Jesus loved her all the more.**

7. She was really taken aback by what Jesus said to her. She thought He was a prophet. She told Him, "The Messiah is coming, and when He comes, He will tell us all things." What was His reply to her? (John 4:26).

8. When she finally realized she was talking with the Messiah, she was so full of joy! She hurried to run back and tell everyone she knew, and what did she leave behind? (John 4:28).

She had encountered the "living water" and she wasn't concerned with the water from Jacob's well in light of everything that just occurred. The story goes on to tell us that many of the Samaritans believed in Him because of her testimony and many more because of His own word.

She saw herself dirty, **but Jesus saw her clean.**

She saw herself unworthy, **but Jesus saw her worthy.**

She saw herself condemned, **but Jesus saw her virtuous.**

9. In regard to your story, in what ways can you relate with the woman at the well?

10. How does this story bring you comfort?

11. Jesus has also traveled to see you. He sees you. He loves you. Allow Him to speak to you now. What is He saying to you?

Jesus spoke healing and life into the Samaritan woman. She had been rejected by everyone, but not by the Messiah, and now she was set free to go and tell the world what He had done for her! She found her significance in Him, and became significant.

If God has given us a gift, it's never for ourselves.

Now, we begin to turn our attention to the next step, offering back to God. God gave the woman at the well a gift. If God has given us a gift, it's never for ourselves. It's always to be offered back to Him by sharing it with others, which in turn can impact the world.

One day I was sitting alone with God and I began to have a vision of a bowl I was tightly gripping and holding close to me. The bowl was overflowing with broken pieces—the broken pieces of my heart. I began to cry and felt this overwhelming desire to extend my arms and offer this bowl back to the Lord. It is a process for sure, but when we can get to the point that we can surrender and offer our brokenness back to Him as a gift, He in return will give us a gift much greater.

Once I saw a graphic of a little girl with brunette hair. She looked sad and she was holding a beat-up, torn little teddy bear. Standing in front of her was Jesus. He was urging her to give Him her teddy. She didn't want to. She wanted to hold onto her teddy, but Jesus kept gently urging her, because behind His back was another teddy bear which He wanted to give her in exchange. What she couldn't see was that the teddy bear behind His back was triple in size, brand new, and beautiful to the eye.

I found myself relating to this little girl and I am so thankful for what this picture represents. Even now, I am clinging to the promise of what Jesus will give me in return for my broken teddy, my broken heart. He loves to give us gifts and treasures to nurture our significance. He wants us to know how much He loves us and values us. He wants us to know how significant we are to the kingdom, and if we are honest, we hunger for it.

God created you to have a hunger for significance. Many look for significance in all the wrong places, but our significance is only found in Him and through our identity in Him. For His glory, He gives us opportunities to express that significance through serving Him and others.

Your significance in Him is what will impact the lives of those around you, just as we see from the story of the woman at the well. Think about this for a moment. The gift God has hiding behind His back for you is for the sake of the world. Whoa! Talk about significance!

The God of the universe chose us!

You did not choose me, but I chose you
and appointed you so that you might go and
bear fruit—fruit that will last—and so

that whatever you ask in my name
the Father will give you.
—JOHN 15:16 NIV

Praise be to the God and Father of our
Lord Jesus Christ, who has blessed us in
the heavenly realms with every spiritual
blessing in Christ. For he chose us in him
before the creation of the world to be holy
and blameless in his sight. In love he
predestined us for adoption to sonship
through Jesus Christ, in accordance
with his pleasure and will.
—EPHESIANS 1:3–5 NIV

CHAPTER 9

The Release

Now is your time of grief, but I will see
you again and you will rejoice, and no
one will take away your joy.

—JOHN 16:22 NIV

R elease means to be set free from confinement, to flow freely. Isn't that a wonderful thought? Grieving and letting go are huge parts of healing. Grieving is a natural and necessary response to pain. Painful circumstances and losses can leave you broken in many ways. Don't believe the lie that you don't have the right to grieve. This chapter speaks the truth that regardless of any painful outcome, it is God's will that you be healed! God is deeply concerned about the broken hearts of his children and He seeks to restore them.

Let's first talk about what grief is. Grief is deep sorrow, especially caused by someone's death, but also arises when we have any significant loss in our lives. Grief feels like a devastating storm that impacts in crashing intervals. At times it feels like a tsunami. A wave comes. It knocks you down. You can't catch your breath. You get back up only to be knocked down again.

Your body aches, your soul aches, your heart aches. Everything looks and sounds foreign.

The world doesn't look and feel the same. It is like you are in a strange place, with familiar faces. A part of you is here, yet a part of you is gone. You try to function, but you discover there are new limitations within you. A different you. There are times when you just space out and can't formulate words. You try to explain what you are going through, but you can't. Many around you don't understand unless they have been through it themselves.

Release means to be set free from confinement, to flow freely.

It is important to understand that grieving is different for everyone and should be honored. It is a highly individual experience. There is no right or wrong way to grieve. There are many factors to consider, like your personality, your coping style, your faith, and how significant the loss was to you. The more significant the loss, the more intense your grief will be. Grieving is a process. Healing takes time and happens gradually. It can't be forced or rushed. No one person grieves the same because no one person is the same. However, we all go through the same stages of grief, which are denial, anger, bargaining, depression, and acceptance. We experience shock, guilt, regret, and other unexpected emotions, especially when it is an unexpected loss.

Also, there is no time limit on grief. For some it may be short, for others longer, but it is okay. What is important is that each individual is moving through the process and not getting stuck. What you don't want to do is sweep the broken pieces under the rug and try and move on with life. This response is not good for you or those around you. You need a lasting healing, so grief has to be properly dealt with.

Many times, counseling is needed to help with the process,

especially if trauma is involved—and let's face it, for most, death is trauma. Many say the wrong things, but out of good intent, so you just do your best to extend grace upon grace. You look for safety and many times you find that alone. It's difficult to go out into the world, so you don't for a season of time. These are all normal responses to grief. It's okay.

I recommend anyone going through grief to have an accountability partner who understands what you are going through. This person can pray for you and help coach you along. I had many accountability partners. I had friends who had gone through grief themselves, some who were just appointed by the Lord. I had a God-sent cousin who brought great comfort and understanding, biblical counselors, and healthcare friends that would just ask simple questions like: Did you eat today? Did you hydrate? Did you rest? All were a gift from God.

> *Two are better than one, because they have*
> *a good return for their labor: If either of*
> *them falls down, one can help the other up.*
> *But pity anyone who falls and has no*
> *one to help them up.*
> —ECCLESIASTES 4:9–10 (NIV)

We were never meant to walk through things alone. Community brings healing. There will be times to be alone with God, and times you need to be in fellowship. God will guide you step by step and pace you through the process, but it's important to keep wise counsel around you. Of course, the greatest counselor can be found here in Psalm 23 (NKJV).

The Lord *is* my shepherd;
I shall not want.

He makes me to lie down in green pastures;

He leads me beside the still waters.
He restores my soul;
He leads me in the paths of righteousness
For His name's sake.
Yea, though I walk through the valley of the shadow of death,
I will fear no evil;
For You *are* with me;
Your rod and Your staff, they comfort me.
You prepare a table before me in the presence of my enemies;
You anoint my head with oil;
My cup runs over.
Surely goodness and mercy shall follow me
All the days of my life;
And I will dwell in the house of the Lord
Forever.

Now, let's return back to the word "release." Release allows the grief permission to move and flow freely. Release is giving your loss back to the Lord, the maker of heaven and earth. Release is giving your loss back to its rightful owner.

This process will allow you to acknowledge and honor your loss and pain, and release it, believing it has great purpose. It also gives great hope and a promise that we will see these purposes fulfilled on earth and heaven. God allows us this experience in a healthy, tangible way so we can settle matters in our heart, release the past, and peacefully move into a bright future.

One thing that helped me tremendously is putting my focus on heaven, our eternal home. I began to shift my focus and thoughts from my sorrow and earthly loss to Christ, eternity, and my loved ones waiting for me in heaven. As I did this, I began to experience inspiration, joy, and peace as I focused on the promises of God. I began to desire heaven more than ever before, wanting to learn as much as I could. I developed more of an eternal perspective and how heaven was impacting my purpose still left on earth. I received a revelation of how the two were working together.

Our present sufferings only point to our future glory!

1. What does Romans 8:18 ask us to consider?
2. What promise is revealed in Psalm 147:3?
3. Who will be comforted in Matthew 5:4?

God's comfort is always on time. He knows just what we need, how we need it, and when we need it.

A Time for Everything (Ecclesiastes 3:1–13 NIV)
There is a time for everything,
and a season for every activity under the heavens:
> a time to be born and a time to die,
> a time to plant and a time to uproot,
> a time to kill and a time to heal,
> a time to tear down and a time to build,
> a time to weep and a time to laugh,
> a time to mourn and a time to dance,
> a time to scatter stones and a time to gather them,
> a time to embrace and a time to refrain from embracing,
> a time to search and a time to give up,
> a time to keep and a time to throw away,
> a time to tear and a time to mend,
> a time to be silent and a time to speak,
> a time to love and a time to hate,
> a time for war and a time for peace.

What do workers gain from their toil? I have seen the burden God has laid on the human race. He has made everything beautiful in its time. He has also set eternity in the human heart; yet no one can fathom what God has done from beginning to end. I know that there is nothing better for people than to be happy and to do good while they live. That each of them may eat and drink, and find satisfaction in all their toil—this is the **gift** of God.

This is your appointed time. A **gift** from God, a time to be still, a time to heal.

The following love letter applies to you if you have experienced the loss of a loved one. However, it contains solid truths to cling to regardless of the source of your pain.

Love Letter #8

My Dearest Child,

Your citizenship is in heaven! Your loved ones are walking the shores of heaven. They are praying for you and look forward to seeing you again someday, but for now, I still have things for you to do here on earth. Seek Me and I will tell you things you do not know (Jer. 33:3).

My child, I will transform lowly bodies and they will be glorious bodies. I have promised you so (Phil. 3:20–21). Grieving is a natural response. It is part of the healing I bring. It is time to release what you have been holding on to so tightly. Give it to Me. As you focus your eyes on Me, on heaven, and on My promises, the pain will lighten and I will heal you, and I will fill you with joy. For behold! I am making all things new!

Do not lose heart. Though outwardly we are wasting away, yet inwardly I renew you day by day. For your light and momentary troubles are achieving for you an eternal glory that far outweighs them all. So, fix your eyes not on what is seen, but on what is unseen, since what is seen is temporary, but what is unseen is eternal (2 Cor. 4:16–18).

Love,

Your Heavenly Father

CHAPTER 10

The Gift I'll Never Forget

But grace was given to each one of us
according to the measure of Christ's gift.
—EPHESIANS 4:7 ESV

few years ago, I was sitting alone with God. I sensed an
internal struggle and I was asking Him to reveal to me
what it was. Then I heard, "You have been believing the
lies." I was then prompted by the Holy Spirit to write down the
things I had been believing about myself. Some of the things
I listed were: lost, forgotten, insignificant, doubtful, rejected,
guilty. As I stared at the words, I heard the Lord say, "Get a permanent marker and X out these things," which I did. Then He
said, "Now, let Me tell you who you really are. Write these words
down." Then I began to hear words that were the opposite of the
words I had originally written down. Words like: found, known,
significant, secure, accepted, free. During this encounter, I was
rediscovering myself in Christ.

This was something of a shock to me. My belief system when
it came to my identity was very superficial and in word only. I
had not allowed the truth to invade my thoughts and heart.
There were layers of unworthiness and false identity that had to

be stripped away. God continually ministered to me. He taught me to "be" instead of "do." To just be still, be His child, be a wife, be a mother, instead of so much doing. I was doing myself to death. Doing ministry, doing work, doing, doing, doing. I wanted God to be proud of me, but guess what, He already was! We don't have to do anything to earn His favor or approval and His approval is the only one that matters!

This may seem like a simple thing, but it can be hard to grasp and apply, because of years of wrong thinking and a false belief system.

God revealed to me that I was basing my identity upon the approval of others. So, when others did not approve of me, I became paralyzed. The truth was that I already had the approval of the King! When I truly accepted this, it was life-changing and suddenly the approval of others quickly faded. I discovered rest and grace like I had never known. There were many gifts I had received from God, but awakening me to my royal identity was a gift I would never forget.

Knowing fully who you are and whose you are becomes the greatest gift of all, a gift you'll never forget.

God looks upon you as the apple of His eye. He sees a treasure, a reflection of His Son. He marvels over you, sings over you. There are no blemishes, only beauty and righteousness, because you are His child. It is this identity that everything must flow from in your life. Then you will enter into more joy, rest, and peace.

That is what this last chapter, this final gift, is all about: securing you in your identity. It is what the enemy runs scared of. He doesn't want you to walk in your identity and speak your identity, because he knows that when you do, you will reflect the image of God and he (the enemy) becomes powerless!

Your core beliefs must be solid. They must be rooted and established. These are your identity, purpose, and value. Knowing fully who you are and whose you are becomes the greatest gift of all, a gift you'll never forget. So, let's dig a little bit, plant some seeds, and allow God to establish some healthy, lasting roots!

1. What does I Peter 2:9 say about your identity?
2. What does the Father call you in I John 3:1?
3. Where does Colossians 3:3 say your life is hidden?
4. What does Galatians 2:20 say about your new life?
5. How does God describe His plans and purposes for you in Ephesians 2:10?
6. Who are you heirs with in Romans 8:17?
7. What promise does Romans 8:1 hold?
8. How long has God known you and appointed you in Jeremiah 1:5?
9. Where does Philippians 3:20 say your citizenship is?
10. Who has blessed you and with what in Ephesians 1:3?
11. What does Colossians 2:10 say about you?
12. What kind of Spirit did God give you in 2 Timothy 1:7?
13. What does Ephesians 1:4 say about you?
14. Who does Jesus say you are in Matthew 5:14?
15. The enemy put you in prison, but when Jesus stepped in, what happened? (Galatians 4:7).

There are still so many other Scriptures throughout the Bible proclaiming your identity. Your heavenly Father is pretty proud of you, His creation, His child, and He likes to brag about you. You bring Him glory! I hope you're smiling right now! When the enemy tries to make you doubt who you are, just return to these Scriptures and discover new ones along the way. Saturate your mind with the book of Ephesians. As our journey together comes to an end, I want to share a couple more stories with you.

There was a man who was a neighbor to a famous sculptor. One day a large block of marble was delivered to the sculptor's backyard and as the neighbor watched, the sculptor walked around and around that big piece of stone. Day after day he walked around and around and then one day he began to chip away at the marble. As the neighbor watched he began to see what appeared to be a man's head being formed, and as the days went by, he could see that the sculptor was indeed making a statue of a man.

When the work was finished, the neighbor went over to visit and when he saw the front of the statue, he exclaimed, "Why, that is a statue of Jesus!" Then he asked the question that had been in his mind ever since that piece of marble had been delivered. "Tell me," he said to the sculptor, "why did you spend all that time walking around and around that big piece of marble before you began to work?" The sculptor smiled and replied, "I was looking to see what was inside that piece of marble and when I saw Jesus in there, I just chipped away everything that wasn't Him."

That piece of marble didn't do a thing to help the sculptor. It just rested and let the sculptor do the work. My friend, that is exactly how God desires to deal with you. When He looks at you, He sees Jesus in you and He is chipping away what isn't Him. All He asks of you is that you rest while He works. He is the sculptor and you are the stone. There is nothing for the stone to do but to believe the sculptor is at work. The outcome will be an ever more perfect expression of the life of Jesus through you. (Story taken from *What Must We Do?* by John Kellogg.)

Beloved daughter of the King, you were made to shine from the inside out. No jewel or gem could ever out-sparkle the beauty of Jesus that radiates from who you are! God wants you to understand and accept your place of authority in the kingdom. He wants you to rise up and fulfill your assignment. Our mistakes don't disqualify us; they qualify us. You don't walk in failure; as a child of God, you walk in favor.

The process of healing is not about what you have experienced or done. It is about who God is and what He has done for you. It is all about His mercy, love, grace, and compassion that He has gifted to us all. Your Savior, my Savior, a Savior to the whole world. He gave His life for all mankind. What a gift!

In the future, let this time serve as a powerful testimony, knowing that "we overcome him [Satan] by the blood of the lamb [Jesus] and the word of our testimony" (Rev. 12:11 KJV). Any negative memories will now be replaced with positive memories of what your Savior has done for you and your citizenship in heaven. Now, you are free and released to go help others. Your ability to help them heal springs from where you have been wounded yourself. With that being said, we now can even recognize the wound as a gift.

God has been in the process of healing your wound. Now He is sealing your wound. Consider your faithfulness to the process, and God's faithfulness to you. What does your wound look like now?

Love Letter #9

My Dearest Child,

Well done! This journey is complete, but more journeys await you. "Forget the former things; do not dwell on the past. See, I am doing a new thing! Now it springs up; do you not perceive it?" (Isa. 43:18–19 NIV).

There is an old hymn called, "I Will Change Your Name." It comes from Revelation 2:17 (NKJV): "And I will give him a white stone, and on the stone a new name written which no one knows except him who receives it."

I have changed your name!

You will no longer be called wounded, outcast, lonely, or afraid.

I have changed your name!

You are now glorious, confident, fearless, joyful one, a healed child of God!

I have changed your name!

I have made a way in the desert for you and a stream in the wasteland (Isa. 43:19). Do not circle this mountain anymore, do not wander this desert, and do not go back (Deut. 2:3). Move forward now into a bright future. I have things for you to do. Obey, take My hand; together we will walk across the bridge, over the stream, and into your promised land. I love you. I am so proud of you. Remember, My child, there is nothing that can change My love for you and I am forever with you.

Love,

Your Heavenly Father

I have one last story to share. When I got the call that my daddy was gone, I was in great agony. I was so worried about him spiritually. Daddy accepted Christ at a young age, but because of so much pain and loss, he had become bitter towards life and God. Our conversations through the years left me always to wonder where he stood in his relationship with Him. As I wept, I heard the Holy Spirit whisper, "The letter." I immediately remembered a letter my daddy wrote a few years prior. I had tucked it away in my Bible. As soon as I could get to it, I pulled it out. Here is what it said:

"Jeannie, for all that you've done and for all that you will accomplish in the future, it all started with you. You will say it started with God, but it didn't. It was you. Why? Because God wants His people to start. He's very simple about it. You start, you confess, you ask for salvation, you serve Him, and then He begins. He blesses you; He guides and directs you. He shows you the way. That's when God comes into your life, after you start. If that's not enough, you feel something that streams through your mind and body with shovels and shovels of warm glowing light. It's simply joy inexpressible. You can't explain to a non-believer. But yes, God's a part of good things, but He wants you to start.

He titled the second page of the letter *"Why You're a Champion Christian."*

- *C: Cause others to see how Satan causes destruction to one's life.*
- *H: Having knowledge in the face of adversity, showing others THE WAY.*
- *A: Anchored in your belief and show goodness to those hurting.*

- M: *Making a smile come to a hurting face, because you helped them.*
- P: *Professing the good and abundant reasons why life should continue.*
- I: *Insurance in the Lord's words.*
- O: *Own your will, the greatest power your mind will ever know.*
- N: *Never forgetting, never forgetting who you are and whose you are.*

Little did I know when I tucked that letter in my Bible that it would become such a treasured gift to me. You see, when I received it years prior to Daddy's death, I seemed to miss the message in it. I came to realize that God was saving it for me when I would need it most. When I read it, I knew my daddy was in heaven with Jesus and agony lifted. There is no way a lost man could have written these words, only a man who knew his Savior personally.

I also realized that Daddy's definition of a Champion Christian was what he was experiencing and witnessing through me. It could have been the very thing that turned his heart back to God. I'm crying even as I write these words, because God is speaking to me and giving me yet another gift. He answered my prayers for Daddy and He let me play a part in it.

You see, I was angry when God took Daddy. I didn't have him growing up, and years later, too soon after we reconciled, God took him. So, I felt like I had been robbed of him twice. What I grieved more than anything was the future I longed for with him. When he was gone, and I realized how depressed he had been, I was saddened that I was not able to help him, but as Daddy described why I was a Champion Christian, I realized that I was helping him all along and I didn't even realize it.

So, never underestimate the influence you could be having on those around you. Letting others see Christ in you could save their lives. Even though Daddy was taken from me twice here on earth, we will now spend eternity together. If our gospel is hidden, it is hidden from those that are lost (2 Cor. 4:3). We must extend the same grace God extends to us or others may never know the gift of new life in Christ.

I discovered that my gift of writing came from Daddy. What a gift it is to share his story with you. It gives me the opportunity to leave a spiritual legacy for him.

I would have never imagined that after losing my daddy in 2020, I would soon lose my grandmother in 2022, and then in less than two months after her death, lose my only biological sibling, my baby brother, at the young age of 43. Both my grandmother and brother passed away during the publishing of this book. In fact, I found myself having to revise the book more than once to be current, transparent, and relevant to where I was seasonally. When I started this assignment, I never imagined I would walk through such grief, but God knew. In fact, working through it, I kept sensing it was not fully complete. I submitted the manuscript and pulled it back numerous times. Now, I know why. I would be hit by tremendous waves of grief. I would get back up from one wave only to be knocked down again.

I have been devastated by the loss of my brother. We were extremely close and our souls always connected. I miss him dearly. I miss his voice and his sweet, pure smile. I have had many questions. Some the Lord may answer. Some He may not, but it will fully be revealed in heaven. I am going through the stages of grief once again, but I cling to the fact that God is good. My brother's earthly death was not God's best for my brother and it was not God's best for me and my family. However, because God is good, He will work all of this together for good (Rom. 8:28).

Again, just like my daddy, I discovered many gifts my brother left behind, particularly his writings. He also had a gift with words. Although there has been great sorrow, I have also been fully inspired to share some of his writings and his personal testimony with the world. I always thought he would bear witness of his own story on earth, because I believed there was a ministry call on his life.

As it turns out, we are going to do this work together. As he is fulfilling his purpose in heaven, his sister will be fulfilling it on earth. We are finally doing ministry together, which was a prayer of mine. He is serving in the spiritual realm and I in the earthly realm.

God has given me my next book to write. I'm going to have a little help from heaven. In the meantime, I will continue to walk in all the same truths I have shared with you throughout this book.

I have been taking you through a process that has three foundations. These three things are the pillars of my ministry to help others discover healing and apply it to their lives so they can soar into purpose. I want to define these for you: First is relational evangelism, which you find through Jesus, and maybe even found through me in the pages of this book. We connect with other people, with their stories of brokenness and restoration. Relationship is the key. Community brings healing. You were never meant to walk the broken road alone. Second is whole healing. Christ desires for you to be healed emotionally, physically, and spiritually. Third is spiritual legacy. Take what God has done for you and share it with the world.

Through a relationship, you were healed, and now as you offer healing to others you will leave a spiritual legacy too. What a beautiful thing! Through our lives, our stories, we see the ripple effect of the gospel taking place. It has been my honor to partner with you through this process.

One day you will tell your story of how you
overcame what you went through and it will
be someone else's survival guide.
—BRENE BROWN

May the Lord bless you
and keep you;
The Lord make His face shine on you
and be gracious to you;
May the Lord turn his face toward you
and give you peace.
—NUMBERS 6:24–26 (NIV)

I love you, friend. I see you. Keep moving forward. Be confident of this, "That he who began a good work in you will carry it on to completion until the day of Christ Jesus" (Phil. 1:6 NIV).

Heaven

Since, then, you have been raised with Christ,
set your hearts on things above, where Christ
is, seated at the right hand of God. Set your
minds on things above, not on earthly things.

—COLOSSIANS 3:1–2 (NIV)

Heaven. A word that just seems to fully complete a sentence. "What a beautiful day it will be when my Jesus I shall see, when He takes me by the hand and leads me to the promised land. What a day it will be when my loved ones I shall see. What a day, a glorious day, that will be."

C.S. Lewis said, "Most of us find it very difficult to want 'heaven' at all—except in so far as 'heaven' means meeting again our friends who have died. One reason for this difficulty is that we have not been trained: our whole education tends to fix our minds on this world. Another reason is that when the real want for 'heaven' is present in us, we do not recognize it."

Possibly due to all the grief I have endured, I have come to recognize my want for heaven as C.S. Lewis wrote about. I am finding that my focus is on heaven more than it ever has been before. I sense a fresh, new perspective of our eternal home and who, and what, awaits us there. Should it not be so? If Christ is in us, heaven is in us. This truth creates a profound realization of how connected we truly are to heaven. As believers living on the earth, by nature it is easy to be consumed or focused on what is around us, things we can actually see.

A question began to arise in my heart. Why do we not spend every waking moment focused on heaven, the place we are going, our home, rather than this world? I began to think on how much healthier I would be physically and spiritually if my focus was there more than it was on the things of this world. I began to realize when my thoughts were on heaven, my loved ones awaiting me there, Jesus, and God in all His glory, that I began to be filled with peace.

This becomes difficult in the flesh, because we live in the world, we are functioning here, and we haven't received the full revelation yet. However, Jesus said, "they are not of the world and do not belong to the world, just as I am not of the world and do not belong to it" (John 17:6 AMP). We are also told in Romans 12:2, "Be not conformed to this world." So, although we live in this world physically, we are set apart spiritually with all spiritual blessings. In Ephesians 2:6 (KJV), it reads, "God has raised us up together, and made us sit together in heavenly places." So, what does this all mean to you and me today?

It means we are in two places at one time. It means we are physically present on earth and spiritually present in heaven. It means we have access to King Jesus and the abundance of heaven. It means that we have the authority of heaven living within us. It means there is a work being done on earth that is affecting heaven, and a work in heaven that is affecting earth. There is an ever-flowing connection. Yes, we are more connected than we may think. The spiritual realm is all around us.

Father, give us eyes to see and hearts to believe. To prove my point, slowly read the prayer Jesus told us to pray. Now, most everyone is familiar with this passage. We have quoted it as young children, during bedtime prayers and beyond, but ask God for a fresh perspective of the words and you will see the connection.

> *Our Father, who art in heaven, hallowed*
> *be thy name; thy kingdom come; thy will*
> *be done; on earth as it is in heaven. Give us*
> *this day our daily bread and forgive us our*
> *trespasses, as we forgive those who trespass*
> *against us. And lead us not into temptation;*
> *but deliver us from evil. For thine is the*
> *kingdom, the power and the glory,*
> *forever and ever, amen.*
>
> −MATTHEW 6:9-13

His will is being done on earth and heaven at the same time. I am going to go a little further and share with you that God is revealing to me our gifts and talents will be used in heaven just as they have been on earth. We are not just going to check out here and do nothing there. Our spiritual gifts in which He alone has given us are just that, gifts! To be used on earth and in heaven.

All the wonders of heaven await us and if we position our-selves to hear and see more of heaven on earth, we will. Life is but a vapor. We are told in James 4:14 (NIV), "Why, you do not even know what will happen tomorrow. What is your life? You are mist that appears for a little while and then vanishes." Friends, there is only one thing keeping us from experiencing ALL heaven has to offer and its glory, and that is our final breath. Until then, we carry on fulfilling our earthly purpose.

We have such a short time here, and all of eternity there if you are a believer and have received Jesus Christ as your personal Savior. Do not delay if you have not. Time is short. I opened this book with an invitation to receive the greatest gift ever given to mankind, and now I want to close doing the same. It will be the most important decision you will ever make. Simply pray:

"Lord, forgive me of my sins. Thank You for paying the ultimate price on the cross so that I may be forgiven and live eternally. I receive this gift and ask that You come into my heart and life and reign. I will follow You. In Jesus' name. Amen!"

If you prayed that prayer, congratulations! Your name is now written in the Lamb's Book of Life. You are a sealed possession. You are eternity-bound! One day we will all enter our permanent home. Jesus, along with our loved ones, will greet us and celebrate our arrival. We will experience the fullness of His perfect love. Until then, awake each morning and say "Good morning, heaven!" They are watching us run our spiritual race as we draw closer to our ultimate purpose. The cloud of witnesses is cheering us on. They are closer than you think.

Throughout the life of Jesus everything He said and done was of utmost importance . . . **for what purpose?**

His took His mouth, time, heart, knowledge, and wisdom and gave His best every day for us to understand . . . **for what purpose?**

He built this land, man and woman, all designed by His hand and all creatures that dwell within . . . **for what purpose?**

Here is the Purpose...

Everything He has done from beginning to end was for us to understand, to live and love by the will of God. The sacrifices He made for us, and our sins. **So, it's through**

Him we have a much larger purpose in life and it's called eternity."

—BENNIE EUGENE SCOTT

Since, then, you have been raised with
Christ, set your hearts on things above,
where Christ is, seated at the right hand of
God. Set your minds on things above, not on
earthly things. For you died, and your life
is now hidden with Christ in God. When
Christ, who is your life, appears, then you
also will appear with him in glory.

—COLOSSIANS 3:1–4 (NIV)

IF YOU'RE A FAN OF THIS BOOK, WILL YOU HELP ME SPREAD THE WORD?

There are several ways you can help me get the word out about the message of this book...

- Post a 5-Star review on Amazon.
- Write about the book on your Facebook, Twitter, Instagram, LinkedIn – any social media you regularly use!
- If you blog, consider referencing the book, or publishing an excerpt from the book with a link back to my website. You have my permission to do this as long as you provide proper credit and backlinks.
- Recommend the book to friends – word-of-mouth is still the most effective form of advertising.
- Purchase additional copies to give away as gifts.

Connect with me at jeanniescottsmith.com

ENJOY THESE OTHER BOOKS
BY JEANNIE SCOTT SMITH

Shattered into Beautiful

Delivering the Brokenhearted from Abortion

Do you want to be restored after abortion? Do you want your mirror to reflect an inner beauty that has been missing? It is time for you to be free. Come receive your miracle!

If You Love Me Obey Me

The Secret to Purpose and Freedom

Moses was entirely human, but was used by God to lead the children of Israel. What was the secret to why God used him in such an amazing way? It lies in his willingness to obey God! Even the wind and the sea obey Him. Will you?

Made in His Image

The Creation of You

Psalm 139 explores our most precious gift: our relationship with God. Soak in the love of the Father as you journey through Psalm 139.

You can order these books from Amazon, Barnes & Noble, or where ever you purchase your favorite books.

NEED A DYNAMIC SPEAKER
FOR YOUR NEXT EVENT?

Connect with me or schedule me to speak at
www.jeanniescottsmith.com